STANLEY BANKS
"First My Friend"

Stanley Banks 1917-1990

STANLEY BANKS
"First My Friend"

RHODA BANKS

OMS INTERNATIONAL
Manchester, England

Copyright © Rhoda Banks 1992

First published 1992

ISBN 0 9250091 0 2

All rights reserved.
No part of this publication may be reproduced or
transmitted in any form or by any means, electronic or
mechanical, including photocopy, recording, or any
information storage and retrieval system, without
permission in writing from the publisher.

Except where indicated otherwise, Scripture quotations are from
the Authorised Version. Crown copyright.

Permission to quote poems from
Amy Carmichael's *Towards Jerusalem*, has been
kindly granted by the SPCK and the Dohnavur Fellowship.

OMS INTERNATIONAL, INC:

World Headquarters, Box A, Greenwood, Indiana 46142, USA
PO Box 195, North Essendon, Victoria 3041, Australia
Box 5222, Station E, Hamilton, Ontario L8S 4L3, Canada
GPO 962, Hamilton, New Zealand
PO Box 640, Roodeport, Transvaal 1725, South Africa

Production and Printing in England for
OMS INTERNATIONAL
1 Sandileigh Avenue, Manchester M20 9LN by
Nuprint Ltd, Station Road, Harpenden, Herts AL5 4SE.

*To
Rachel, Ian, Stuart
and Meryl*

Contents

Foreword by Dr Denis Applebee		11
Introduction		13
1	Early Years	17
2	Training for Service	27
3	The Years in the Work of Emmanuel	37
4	Minister-at-Large	51
5	'Not Just a Teacher…'	63
6	Man and Message	71
7	To The Uttermost Parts…	87
8	Joy of Life and Family	95
9	The Last Lap	111

FOREWORD

ABOVE THE ROSTRUM of the main lecture hall of Emmanuel College, Birkenhead, were the framed words of Jonah 3:2, 'Preach the preaching I bid thee!' The implication that every time we stand behind the sacred desk we must know it is God's message for the hour filled me with awe. It still does! It seemed to me that every time I heard Stanley Banks preach, he knew his message to be God's word for the hour. With quiet dignity and a God-given authority, he presented expositions of the word. They were always that, and they were also logical in outline and analytical in content. As a lecturer in homiletics, he certainly preached what he taught; and as a preacher, he lived what he preached.

Son-in-law of the founder of Emmanuel College, he stepped into J.D. Drysdale's shoes with a perfect fit. Two men, though so very different, yet both walking in step with the Spirit, led to a work which saw hundreds of students pass through their hands out into ministries around the world. As one of those students,

I had the privilege of sitting under his ministry, then working alongside him and finally being his successor in pastorate and leadership. This gave me the opportunity to see Stanley Banks, the man, and benefit from his ministry and wise counsel over many years.

Those years spanned the middle of this century, a time of great changes. He adapted to them by ministering to the needs of people in such scripturally based messages that his work was never dated. He taught in lands around the globe and in cultures foreign to his own. He ministered by radio to Africa and by print from his memorable convention addresses. All were and are relevant. That is why, as you will read in this book of personal memories of this man of God, he was able to minister to missionaries and miners, seminary students and laymen alike. His feet were always on the ground, but his messages were always heaven-approved. He preached the preaching he was bidden.

I am delighted that this account of his life is published during the lifetime of those who knew Stanley Banks best, but in years to come it will remain a challenge to preachers to seek always to be under the anointing which alone comes when we preach as bidden. It is with a sense of honour and debt that I write this foreword and recommend to you the reading of this story. To know Stanley Banks was to love him, respect God's word through him, and to know a friendship that challenged many lives deeply to reflect the life he lived and the Saviour he loved.

Denis Applebee

INTRODUCTION

MANY READERS SUGGESTED to me that I should give you Stanley's story in a permanent form. For over a year after God called him home I felt myself to be inadequate, for many reasons, to make such a contribution to such a life. I felt it would be impossible to show you in mere words what a very special person he really was. I felt even that some of you might be disappointed to find out that he was after all just a 'saint in work clothes' (the title of a book he wrote on the work of the Holy Spirit in the life of the believer), rather than a saint on a pedestal; that he enjoyed watching a cricket match, not just spending hours studying God's word; or that he appreciated the finer points of a good brass band performance even though he also sang the Songs of Zion with such heart and gusto.

But the inner insistence of the Holy Spirit underlined the requests from his and my friends, so with trepidation and yet a sense of privilege, I give you this story of Stanley, an ordinary man, a miner's son from a

Derbyshire village, who left school at fourteen, without so much as a single academic qualification; who went to no earthly university, gained no degree; who laughed at anyone anywhere who mistakenly and even stubbornly insisted on calling him 'Doctor': but special in the way that everyone of us is special to God; one who let God possess him, not in any sense a perfect man, one with ordinary faults and failures, but one who never set out to be what he wasn't; one who could laugh at himself and could enjoy the jokes of others against himself; one who never felt he had arrived, but continued to learn and grow, as he beheld 'as in a mirror the radiant holiness of the Lord, being transformed from one degree of radiant holiness to another, as by the Lord, the Spirit' (this quotation from Weymouth's translation of 2 Corinthians 3:18 was one he often used and preached on). He was one who showed us Jesus in each part of his life.

His elder daughter, Rachel, put this into poetic picture during the hours of the long night after her father went to heaven:

Daddy:
You gave me life.
You lived before me as God's man,
You showed me Jesus.

Remember Christmas's fun and games?
You showed me Jesus.

Remember holidays, walks, swimming, laughter and enjoyment?
You showed me Jesus.

Introduction

Remember teens, with problems and pains?
You showed me Jesus.

Remember courtship, engagements and weddings?
You showed me Jesus.

Remember grandchildren, spoiling and hugging?
You showed me Jesus.

Remember separations, long and short, far and near?
You showed me Jesus.

And now you're with Him: you still show me Jesus.
My thanks to God for showing me Jesus in you.

In the telling of his story I want to thank those who have helped by adding your memories of Stanley to mine (so many that the question throughout the writing has not been what to include, but what to leave out). Thanks also to my family, who have contributed and encouraged me; to a friend in my home village who offered, unexpectedly and unsolicitedly, to do the word-processing; to Emmanuel Bible College, OMS and to many others who have made the publication possible; but above all to the One who brought us together in the first place, and to whom we owe everything.

Rhoda Banks

CHAPTER

1

EARLY YEARS

Stanley at 17 years old.

It was the 18th May, 1990. We were busy and happy as we prepared to go to Scotland for a holiday in a self-catering country cottage, to be followed by a week's lecturing to the students of the Faith Mission Bible College in Edinburgh. Our shopping finished at the supermarket (each choosing our 'favourite things') we returned home to complete our packing for the next day's journey and to tidy up the garden. Then as he trimmed the edges of our tiny lawn at the back of the cottage, Stanley heard the summons to the immediate presence of his Lord. His passing into that Presence could not have been briefer or more sudden. As I knelt beside him on the ground, I knew that those eyes (on earth, so very blue and always tender and smiling) had already looked on the face of the One he had loved and served single-heartedly for many years.

Eternal realities seemed very close in the time that followed. Within a few hours all our family were with me, and we had never been as close in heart to each other as we were then. The atmosphere in the home was something very sacred and alive with His comforting presence, so much so that one member of the family whispered, as she said goodbye after the triumphant funeral (which was far more like a celebration): 'It's been like a little bit of heaven.'

About sixty years earlier two young teenagers sat together in a small Methodist Chapel in a Derbyshire mining village listening spell-bound to an ex-missionary from China as she pressed upon her congregation the claims of Christ and the challenge of following him. At the close of her message she appealed especially to the young people to give their lives wholly to him. Amongst several others, John, aged 16, and Stanley, aged 14, jumped from their seats and went to the front. The ex-missionary, then known as 'Sister May', a Methodist deaconess, prayed with them in the vestry and led them to Christ. Stanley's grandfather, William Salway, then took the two boys back into the church, quietly insisting that they tell the congregation what God had done for them, thus 'nailing their colours to the mast'.

This was where it all began: Stanley's life-long commitment to his Lord and Master.

Stanley Banks, an only child, was born in 1917 in Hepthorne Lane, Clay Cross, a suburb of Chesterfield, which at one time proudly proclaimed itself as 'the heart of industrial England'. His mother, Annie Salway, was born into a godly home; her father, William Salway, although he left school at 14, further educated himself, eventually becoming chairman of the local Education Committee, a Justice of the Peace and, above all, a powerful preacher of the gospel. Annie was a born actress and comedienne who could keep an audience entertained and creased with laughter by a solo performance. She went her own way, marrying Ernest Banks, a young army officer, in 1914. Together they certainly gave lip-service to the Methodist Church, but their lives were ruled by bridge parties, performing in concert parties and a very active social life in which Christ's claims went unanswered. During a very serious, life-threatening illness, when Stanley was 13 years of age, his mother was brought face to face with her own deep spiritual need of a personal Saviour and came out of hospital a changed person. Life in the home for Stanley and his father was radically changed, too, for it was now a divided home, father and son going their own accustomed way of life without Christ, while the mother's life now had a totally new centre and impetus, her whole desire focusing on the day when the family would again be united, but this time in Christ.

It must have been a very difficult time for her, but the consistency of her Christian witness and the sincerity of the change of direction in her life was so obvious that one Sunday morning, a year later, Stanley's father asked her to pray with him and lead him to Christ.

Stanley knew something unusual must be happening, for in such a well-regulated, punctual family, breakfast was never late. He sat waiting, waiting, until

EARLY YEARS

Stanley's Father, Ernest Banks, as a young officer.

eventually his father, by this time a hard-headed, hard-swearing colliery official, came down to the breakfast table, tears streaming down his face (Stanley used to say he had never seen his father cry in all his life) and falteringly said, 'Son, your mother's led me to Christ.'

So now it was Stanley who was the odd one out in the home. For a year he watched. A new atmosphere of love and tolerance, prayer and devotion crept into the home, and gradually conviction of his own need of Christ took the place of rebellion and annoyance in his heart. And the night came when, most unenthusiastically, he and his pal, John Turner, went down to the chapel in the little village of Doe Lea to hear 'Sister May'.

John remembers that the meeting was 'electric with the power of the Lord Jesus', so perhaps it was no surprise that John and Stanley and several other young people, all converted that night, formed what they were pleased to call a 'mission band', holding open air meetings in the villages of the Bolsover Circuit, visiting door-to-door, witnessing wherever they went. It was noticeable soon after his conversion that Stanley had a gift of communication as he began to give his 'testimony' at various chapels and house groups.

On leaving school (Queen Elizabeth's Grammar School, in Mansfield) he became an electrical engineering student in the Glapwell Colliery (now no more, having given way for the development of the M1 Motorway), where his father was manager. But he had no preferential treatment because of this fact; he began at the bottom!

During these years he and other young men, among them Harry Bates and a young Leith Samuel (later to become the minister of Above Bar Church,

EARLY YEARS

In a small Methodist Chapel in a Derbyshire mining village, Stanley, aged 16 and John Turner aged 14 accepted the challenge to give their lives to Jesus Christ.

Southampton), gave up their holidays to go 'trekking' around England, evangelising with the League of Prayer, under the leadership of Kenneth Hooker, testifying and preaching to sinner and saint alike.

Soon after their conversion Stanley's parents had been invited to attend the annual missionary convention of the Japan Evangelistic Band (JEB) at the Hayes Conference Centre in Swanwick, Derbyshire. Through this yearly contact a strong missionary influence and burden developed in their lives, so it was a natural progression for the young Stanley to absorb some of their enthusiasm in the early days of his Christian commitment. The JEB ran what was known as the 'Sunrise Band', the branch of the mission geared to young people. Stanley and his teenage friends had formed their own 'band' within this soon after their conversion, receiving regular information about missionary work in Japan, going to JEB conventions at Swanwick, their appetites being stimulated in missionary interest, holding their own prayer meetings for Japan. As his late teenage years came, a burden and vision began to grow in Stanley's heart. He became aware that electrical engineering was not to be his calling, that God was calling him instead to a life of total commitment to his service.

What was to be the next step? Stanley had never had very glowing school reports from Queen Elizabeth's: usually it was a repetitive 'must work harder' or 'Stanley is capable of better than this' or 'His mind is too occupied with sport: he must apply himself to his studies' and so on. For always this man—as a young boy, teenager, young adult, student, teacher, pastor, college principal, missionary and retiree was interested (perhaps the greatest understatement ever!) in sport of all kinds.

His first love in this field was cricket; in his young days he was good enough to play in the junior county cricket and football teams; but he was knowledgeable in any sport. It was noted later in life by the headmaster of Birkenhead School, when we lived near its playing fields, that he had 'unfeigned pleasure in watching the school rugby team' and a 'shrewd assessment of their performance': indeed this could be said of his interest in and knowledge of all kinds. His enthusiasm was infectious and as he watched a game or match on the television he became mentally and often almost physically involved, greatly to the amusement of other watchers! In our retirement days in the little village of Great Barrow in Cheshire, one of his great enjoyments

EARLY YEARS

Worksop Season 1932. Bassetlaw League. Stanley is first on left on front row.

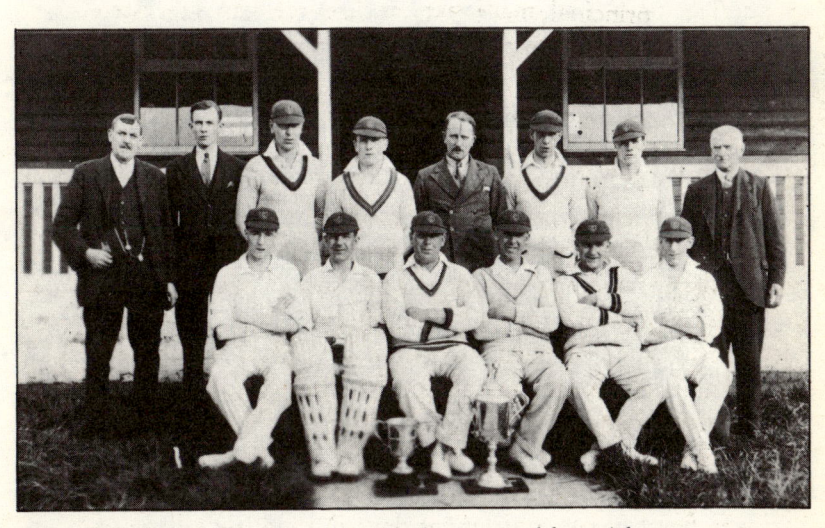

Glapwell Colliery Cricket Team, 1934. Stanley is second from right on front row, and his father fourth from right.

was to play crown green bowls. He made many friends in the Bowling Club (and incidentally made the team too). 'I always felt comfortable with Stanley,' said one of them to me after his homecall. He was known as the 'Rev', and Jack, one of his fellow-bowlers, would say to other players, 'You can't swear when the Rev's here.'

Much as he loved all sport, it was in fact Christ who more and more became the real centre of his life. Thus he began to realise that not only must his heart and life be fully committed, but also that he must prepare his mind, too. For having left school at 14 without any academic qualifications, he was aware of shortcomings in this part of his life. So what was he to do? How prepare himself to be of use to God?

CHAPTER 2

TRAINING FOR SERVICE

Stanley belonged to a large, wider-family circle of cousins on his mother's side, and family life revolved around the grandparents, William and Annie Salway, at the Clay Cross home. 'Get-togethers' at Christmas and holidays were highlights in the family's year. Then later, after Grandfather Salway went to be with the Lord and Grandma came to live with Stanley's parents, the venue for reunions moved to their home in Bramley Vale, the small village near the coal mine and the Doe Lea Chapel. His uncles regularly came to visit Grandma Salway—Stanley loved to describe her as the 'saintliest person he had ever known'—bringing a cousin or two with them. Peter, one of them, remembers that Stanley was a 'laughing, red-cheeked, very friendly cousin'. Phyllis, another cousin, and Stanley often went for holidays to Auntie Clara's at Barnsley, where he had the reputation of being 'quite a mischievous young boy'.

In the unusual circumstances of an entire family which stayed in the same area even into adulthood and old age, it must have seemed to the 18-year old Stanley that he would be the first to break the pattern if he moved away, not only from a close family background, but from the very area of Derbyshire which had always been 'theirs'.

But God's call was becoming insistent in his young heart. His parents, in their total commitment and consecration to Him of their lives, their home, their son, had no wish to hold him back if this call was to be answered. So, as a family, they all began to pray for clear guidance about Bible College training. In today's world, amidst a plethora of colleges of every hue and persuasion, young people have before them screeds of prospectuses, brochures and application forms: they weigh up one college against another, study the facilities available, the environment of each college, its attractiveness at many levels and, above all, which one appeals to them most strongly. Maybe this is right when such a wide choice is available. But in the pre-war years, young would-be students, feeling themselves unmistakably called to missionary service, prayed for clear guidance about which college was for them. They then applied to that one and expected God to make clear to them his will in their acceptance or otherwise by the college concerned.

Ever since his conversion Stanley's heart had been burdened for the needs of Japan and although, as subsequent events were to prove, he did not reach that land as a missionary, he often used to say in later life that God used Japan to stir him out of his home 'nest', to fledge his wings in order to reveal his plan for him.

About this time, the WEC (Worldwide Evangelisation Crusade) sent two of their prospective candidates, Leslie Brierly and Ted Gibbons, to Doe Lea Chapel to tell of their call. Over the weekend of their ministry they stayed in the Banks' home, only briefly, but—as it turned out—significantly. While they were there, the name of their Alma Mater (Emmanuel Bible College, Birkenhead) crept into conversation frequently. These two young men left an exceptionally favourable impression in the home. It could hardly have been imagined what far-reaching repercussions this visit would have. Stanley was deeply impressed by their consistent, happy and sincere lives, and his parents by their thoughtful behaviour in the home and their utter commitment to give their whole lives to Christ's service. After they left his father said to Stanley:

'If Emmanuel' (of which he had never previously heard) 'can produce two young men of that calibre, that's the place for you, son.'

So, some few months later, Stanley arrived with his trunk on the doorstep of Emmanuel Bible College. Did he have any notion of what the future would hold for him in the closest possible ties with EBC? I know he didn't!

His student days may have started in Emmanuel Bible College, but they never ended. His love for studying God's word and the truths it proclaims began in those teenage years but, to the end of his life, one of his greatest joys was to study scriptural truth under the guidance of the Holy Spirit. In his college days he probably had to study to pass exams, but he was a student and a reader to the end. Just before the Lord took him, he was deep in a study of Hebrews, finding fresh gems. Friends came to visit and in greeting them, he burst out, 'I've been studying Hebrews: I must preach it; it is bubbling up inside me.'

At this point I would like to pre-empt something which I will stress later. After he died, hundreds of tributes poured through my letter-box thanking God

Stanley in centre front of group of 1950 students.
Back Row left to right: Jack Sperry, Bob McAllister, Jack Crouch, Wyndham Lewis.
Front Row left to right: Ken Jolley, Reg Davies, Stanley, John Eaves, Len McNeil.

for Stanley's clear, knowledgeable, thorough, balanced and acceptable presentation of the truths of the scriptures, from original sin to holiness, justification to sanctification, interpretation and application, practical living and working...and so much more. But one of his most often used words was 'discipline': and this he learned in his college days. Who has not heard him say, 'God will wake you up in the morning, but he will not get you up; you must do that yourself; there are no ejector seats in the bed.' And how often he told a story of his days as Principal of EBC many years later when, casually entering the students' common room a few days before exams, he surprised a young student stretched out on a settee, a book on his head.

'What on earth are you doing, David?' he asked.

'I'm praying it will soak in,' answered the optimist.

'Wouldn't it be nice,' Stanley used to say, 'if it happened just like that?' But he soon realised, at the commencement of his own training, that God had given him a mind which he himself must apply and use if he wanted rightly to 'divide the word of truth'.

But it was not all study: college days were days of learning in every aspect of life, days of character training, days of practical 'scrubology', as 'chores' of all kinds were known at EBC, days of the formation of friendships which enriched and remained till the end of his life. One remembers him as a 'sincere friend who was just the same when I met him again on his visits to Ulster as when I had last said goodbye to him'. This same friend recalls the times on campaign during vacation when they used to sing together:

I want my life to tell for Jesus
That everywhere I go, men may his fullness know:
I want my life to tell for Jesus.

Another remembers him in the 'old Bible School days, tall, slim, full of life and, it felt, always with that lovely, happy smile'. They were days of fun, too! Stanley himself took a boyish delight in recounting how they dealt with a fellow-student who wouldn't get up in the morning: the treatment, which never needed repeating, consisted of lifting man and mattress, carrying him downstairs, out of the house and dumping him on the lawn.

They were days, too, when deep lessons in 'praying through' were learned; whole nights, early mornings, when many battles were fought and won, lessons learned which were never to be forgotten.

His theological background from the time of his conversion was in the Arminian tradition, and the years spent in EBC confirmed in his heart and mind the wonder and reality of the truths of the Holy Spirit's work in the life of the believer. (Many years later Stanley did an extensive study into the 'Wesleyan heritage' and became an authorititive source of information on the subject.)

It was during student days, as he studied in depth the potential extent of the Holy Spirit's purifying and empowering work, that Stanley himself became increasingly aware of a deep need in his own life; until one day, when praying with a fellow-student, his own powerlessness and need overwhelmed him, and he himself sought the baptism of the Holy Spirit. He claimed the promise in Ezekiel 36:25–27 about cleansing, a new heart and a new spirit which would cause him 'to walk in his way'. He knew this was only the beginning, not an end in itself, and that throughout his life he must for ever 'learn of him' and obey the Spirit's constraints and restraints, humbly admitting and confessing failure or shortcomings. He had not 'arrived', he was but starting out on the 'Golden Highway' of holiness (the title of a book he was later to write on the subject). There were times in his life when he felt the need of confession and repentance—as one colleague recalls:

> I remember the Sunday morning service during an Easter convention when Stanley, in tears, shared with us in the congregation that for quite a time he had had a controversy with the Lord and had been unwilling to obey the Lord, but that now he had yielded, broken before the Lord. From then on I saw that Stanley was a 'broken man' in the Lord's hands and his manner of living exemplified that brokenness to the day of his going to be with the Lord.

In 1938 towards the end of his student days at EBC he applied to the Japan Evangelistic Band for service overseas. At that time much of the work of the JEB was concentrated on evangelism in the rural areas of Japan, and because this type of work was particularly close to Stanley's heart this was the direction of his application to the JEB. The Faith Mission (of Edinburgh, Scotland) reached out in its 'pilgrim' work in the rural districts of the Scottish Highlands and Northern Ireland, so the JEB included in its orientation of candidates for Japan a period out in the villages and country districts of these areas under the Faith Mission's auspices.

So, tentatively accepted by the JEB, Stanley's preparation for service continued in the Highlands of Scotland, first of all in the Black Isle, north of Inverness. I would need to write a separate book to tell you of his many experiences, often challenging, sometimes lonely, sometimes discouraging, many times hilarious—fruitful times too—but always profitable and character-forming, through which he passed in those eighteen months in rural evangelism. The home and family in Munlochy where he was billeted always retained a very special place in his memory, and the daughters of the Miller family, Rita (who later became the wife of Ian Hall of Gideons International) and Gladys, have told me of the example and challenge his life was to them when still in their mid-teens: how he encouraged them in their rather reluctant 'witnessing for Christ' at school. Gladys remembers that 'Rita and I went to the meetings every night in the church hall. I was rebellious in those days and afraid to take my stand for Christ...but years later I appreciated the challenge of his ministry and witness.' And Rita, too, acknowledges that this was the time when the need of India really reached her heart, even though it was Japan which 'he used to talk about a lot'.

His evangelism with the Faith Mission also involved a period in remote Glen Urquhart near Loch Ness, under the wise, adventurous and often 'hare-brained' leadership of Ellis Govan (son of the founder of the Faith Mission). All the house-to-house evangelism had to be done on foot: not even bikes would have been much help in those steep-sided, rugged glens. He learned many more prayer lessons in those days. Ellis would recommend early mornings of prayer. 'Anyone can stay up to pray at night—we'll get up at 5.00am and pray through till midday,' he would say. Sometimes, as a young trainee evangelist would be demanding 'great things' of God in his praying, Ellis would interrupt him: 'Brother, what authority have you to ask God for that?' He would impress upon them that their requests must be based on the promises of God.

So Stanley learned one of the lessons which subsequently throughout his life he put into practice—the importance of taking for his own a promise from God's Word and standing on it.

He always counted it as one of the greatest privileges of his training days that he was sent to the Isle of Lewis in the Outer Hebrides for a period, before the revival which swept the island a few years later. He grew spiritually under the leadership of, and because of his close contact with, Duncan Campbell (used by God in the revival), with whom he formed a relationship of great respect, affection and fellowship. (This lasted for a lifetime, and Stanley had the great joy of returning to Lewis with him in the late 1950s, after the revival.)

But then came the outbreak of war in September 1939 and, as for many people, everything changed.

CHAPTER

3

THE YEARS IN THE WORK OF EMMANUEL

THE LETTER ARRIVED which would change the whole direction of Stanley's life. A closed door to Japan because of the outbreak of war must surely mean that his Lord was about to open another one. But what now? 'Where do I go from here?' he wondered. Throughout his training days in EBC he had greatly revered and been guided by his college principal, the Rev. John D. Drysdale, who had founded the college in 1920. So it seemed the most natural thing in the world that he should seek his advice at this crisis in his life.

So with an open mind and heart, desiring to know God's will, he returned. In after days, when telling of that day, he was heard to say, 'So I went back to my former principal—and I'm still here, X years later.'

It was perhaps the most momentous day of his life.

'We are short of help in the church on the pastoral side and in the college office,' said J.D. (as the principal was always affectionately known by his students— behind his back, of course!). 'So will you stay on in a temporary capacity and help us while you are seeking God's will for the future?'

'Yes,' he replied, little realising where this decision would lead him.

The work of Emmanuel, founded in 1916 by my father and mother, John and Lily Drysdale, began with a church fellowship, firstly in a room over a shop, then moving to a dilapidated old Methodist chapel, and eventually to its present building, known still as Emmanuel Holiness Church, in downtown Birkenhead. This was the church where Stanley began to minister in a part-time capacity in 1940, where he made many lasting friendships and where his spiritual muscles were flexed in preaching, counselling, administration, leading young people's fellowship and Sunday school work. This involvement led, in 1942, to his ordination and induction into the pastorate of the church for the next ten years.

In 1920 the college had come into being as young people in the church felt the call to missionary work overseas, and after many months of prayer for guidance my parents opened the doors of their own home to prepare prospective missionaries for God's calling in their lives. As the numbers of students grew, it became necessary to find a larger building, and the miraculous story of the provision of the present premises has been told elsewhere (*Prophet of Holiness*, by Norman Grubb). God gave a wonderfully committed and sacrificial group of men and women to help John and Lily Drysdale in their task, not merely in the practical administration and general running, but on the academic side too. But the outbreak of war in 1939 produced its own crop of problems for staffing, in every area. So although Stanley's help in the college centred first of all in the office and a thousand-and-one practical

Rhoda's Father.

The Years in the Work of Emmanuel

Rhoda's Mother.

jobs on campus, it was not very long before the principal called Stanley to him one day and announced: 'We need someone to lecture on homiletics. I want you to take this on.'

Stanley would later have great delight, when recounting this incident, in saying: 'Of course, those were the days when the staff and not the students ran the colleges, so of course I just had to get down to it and start to prepare a series of lectures on the given subject; and most of the time I was just one lecture ahead of the students and prayed they would not ask me any questions I couldn't answer.'

Lecturing on Biblical Introduction soon followed his ventures into homiletics and, later still, Biblical Theology. With hindsight, it is hard to imagine how he did it all! And as the years passed and church, pastoral and teaching responsibilities increased, and as administration accelerated and he became the editor of the magazine, *Emmanuel*, it was obvious that he knew an inner strength and enabling. One of his favourite modern translations of Philippians 4:13 was: 'By his dynamic power I am able to cope with any situation.' Lionel Hawker, who joined the Emmanuel family in 1952, has said, 'I am not sure that it always came as easily as it appeared to us, looking on, but that it all seemed so natural helped those of us who worked with him.'

When in 1953 my father received his homecall and Stanley was appointed principal, Lionel Hawker was 'struck by the calmness and confidence with which he faced the future and took over the sole responsibility. Whatever he felt inwardly, he showed little of it to us and was a great encouragement.' Stanley himself was inspired by a Sunday morning message given by Lionel

Hawker in Emmanuel Church on the Sunday after my father died. His text was: 'As I was with Moses, so I will be with you. I will not leave you nor forsake you' (Joshua 1:5).

This is Stanley's story, not mine! But how the Lord brought us into each other's lives and made us one—for our own joy and life together, yes, but chiefly for His ultimate purposes—must be part of this story, too.

As my father's secretary in the college, I spent most of my working hours in the office. So when Stanley told his parents that he felt his heart 'strangely warmed towards Rhoda', he surely knew where to find me. We shared many special secrets in the office, but the day had to come when, as Stanley used to say, he 'faced the most difficult thing he'd yet had to do in his life': to go to his principal and ask for the hand of his daughter in marriage. He has often related how some of the men students to whom he was most close in age and in fellowship, told him to 'go and get it over with and we'll stay here and pray for you'. Evidently their prayers were effective. Consent being given, and both of us feeling assured of God's will in the matter, we were married in Emmanuel Church on June 25th 1942.

The eleven years that followed were very busy, full and constructive in Stanley's life: years when God was preparing him for much that lay in his future, of which he had no idea. Under the principalship and leadership of J.D. Drysdale he absorbed teaching and example constituting a challenge which at times was daunting; often we knew together that it was a challenge neither of us could meet in our own strength. But my father's strong faith and courageous living were a source of great strength and encouragement through these early

Stanley and Rhoda on their wedding day, June 25th, 1942.

The Years in the Work of Emmanuel

Stanley's parents, Ernest and Annie Banks.

Stanley's grandparents, William and Annie Salway.

Stanley and Rhoda with their family in 1964.
Back Row: left to right: Stuart, Stanley, Ian. *Middle Row:* Rachael, Rhoda. *Front:* Meryl.

years of involvement in the college and church. In the early 50s those of us who were closest to him were conscious that my father knew he had not much longer to serve the Lord here on earth. It often puzzled us that he seemed so sure of this fact, but God had endowed him with a unique gift of discernment; especially had this been noticeable in his dealings with students and staff alike, and of course this inspired great trust in those of us around him, as often subsequent events would prove how Spirit-inspired this discernment had been. So although we heard him say he knew he had only a short time left and were reluctant to believe it, we sensed that he was able to discern even at this time in his life what God was revealing to him. So accept it we must! And in the accepting came the discipline of hearts and lives for the greater responsibilities we were to shoulder so soon, proving that 'through his dynamic power I am able to cope with any situation'.

Thus in January 1953 Stanley was appointed principal of EBC, a position he held till 1970.

These years were frought with many of the problems that were the warp and woof of a changing world in the post-war era. But the foundation laid in his first years in EBC stood him in good stead, as he faced the necessity of internal changes in the college. Change is never easy and as crises and problems arose because of the altering climate from which the young people came, 'he acted with confidence and so often seemed able to sense the right action to take and the right thing to say' remembers Lionel Hawker (who, by this time, was pastoring the church as well as lecturing part-time in the college). His discernment showed as he put into motion 'the plans and vision for the redirection and reorganisation of the whole work'. Lionel's wife, Barbara, also spoke of how 'open he was to change, always alert to see how external truth and values could best be made relevant in a changing world, without sacrificing that which is vital. But he would not be pushed into change prematurely.'

Barbara remembers, too, that on one occasion she heard a 'member of staff ask for a concession on a seemingly insignificant matter. His answer was prompt, concise and unambiguous. "The answer is no!" '

His students have spoken of 'his God-appointed exposition of the word', of hearing his voice 'so clear and confident in teaching', of 'the debt we students owe to him', the lectures which were 'so clear I could go on listening', of 'his unique ability to make difficult scriptural doctrines easy to understand', of his 'clear, balanced teaching in the Spirit' and of his 'example of study and preaching, encouraging my slow mind to work'.

But there was another sphere in which the Holy Spirit was educating him for a future ministry as yet unguessed: that of personal counselling and guidance on a wider scale. Stanley never found it easy to 'face people up' with their shortcomings or failures and would sometimes quote Amy Wilson Carmichael of Dohnavur, India, who said, 'If I can hurt another by speaking faithfully without much preparation of spirit and without hurting myself far more than I hurt that other, then I know nothing of Calvary love.' He would sometimes pray that the Lord would send to him those in need, rather than that he should search them out.

Perhaps this very attitude gave others, especially his students, the confidence to approach him; for his advice was ever practical, wise and down-to-earth. 'Let the cross go through your affections,' he would say to someone seeking guidance regarding a questionable friendship. One student found out his approachability when he 'had personal problems and sought his advice. He exhorted me to hand everything over into the hands of God and promised to pray for me'. 'He was a wise and caring counsellor when I came to him in spiritual need.' 'He prayed me through difficult years when I was limping along with my spiritual and not-so-spiritual disturbances—he was so wise and understanding, and yet so faithful.' 'He had a prayerful and powerful concern for each of us.' One spoke of him as 'my spiritual father'.

It seems very probable that much of this approachability came from the fact that, as one Jack Sperry says (who later became Anglican Bishop of the Canadian Arctic Diocese): 'He was one of us.' He remembers that 'to us, on entering EBC, somewhat uncertain about life and discipline in a missionary training college, in Stanley Banks we met one who ministered to us as principal and an interested and approachable friend, one equally at home in the lecture hall as when sharing with the men in an early morning run or a game of football. He was but a few years older than us in those early days and was a down-to-earth Christian brother.'

Again, perhaps it was because his humanity and 'supernatural naturalness' reached through to those around him.

'I remember his grin, as he moved from one foot to the other, in lectures, often delivering some simple, straightforward theological thought that he knew was confusing our little minds.'

'I remember so well his endearing habit of rolling his tie up and down when in conversation.'

'Holiness for him was a way of life, not just some cold doctrine that hit the head without getting down to the heart.'

A fellow member of staff recalls: 'I remember how, in the maintaining of a healthy ethos in the community of students, he could handle things effectively, without fuss and in a few words, even with a humorous touch. One morning at assembly he had one notice to give. He said: "There are two little bugs going around the college. One is called I'm tired; the other is I didn't have time. You won't let them bite you, will you?" That's all; then he walked out. I've never forgotten it, nor the depth of wisdom in it.'

'I have it on good authority,' another has told me, 'that on one occasion Stanley made good use of one of the college's stirrup pumps, using it with effect on some "sister" students! He always made you feel his equal; never did he assume a superior stance, although he merited this position by his quality of life.'

And in our home, during male voice choir practices, several have reminisced about 'getting to know him' in his domestic setting. 'We learned more of the human side of the man, who, to us then was already a spiritual giant, to whom we looked up as we shared humorous banter.'

Maybe this winsome personality can be summed up in the words of Mary Peckham, wife of the Rev. Colin Peckham, principal of the Faith Mission Bible College, when she said, 'He was a happy, jovial, sane and practical saint.'

This 'sane and practical saint' on one occasion asked his students the following questions:

Am I a thermostat (one who affects the atmosphere around him) or a thermometer (one who is affected by the atmosphere around him)?
Do I pray either in private or public only when I feel like it?
Am I irritated and irked by circumstances not to my liking or by the demands of others? If so, why?
Are my attitudes to others always constructive and not destructive?
What benefits have I received from training?...
- Is God more real?
- Is life more disciplined?
- Am I easier to live with?
- Is my spirit humbler?
- Is my life more godly?
- Is my concern for others more potent?
- Am I more submissive or more assertive?

It is possible that these questions are in themselves a commentary on Stanley's thirty-four years with Emmanuel Bible College. And the many experiences through which he passed, the problems faced and solved, the sometimes seemingly insoluble situations, were, as he once said, but a prelude and a preparation for the next chapter of his life.

CHAPTER 4

MINISTER -AT- LARGE

'UNLESS WE ARE UNANIMOUS in our decisions, we don't act.' This had been the pattern the executive council of Emmanuel had adopted through many years—an unwritten law, but one firmly held by an equally unwritten sense of unity and a conviction that God would guide us unfailingly into his will if we sought it honestly.

So when Stanley came one day to an executive council meeting in the late '60s and astonished the gathered brethren by telling them that God was clearly leading him to a wider ministry, he certainly expected them to go along with him in his guidance.

For a year or more the conviction had been growing that the experiences of the thirty years within Emmanuel were instrumental in preparing him for a ministry of teaching and counselling which could reach around the world. He himself had no positive ideas as to how or through what channel this could be, or who would take his place as principal, but God's clear assurance to him was, 'I will bring the blind by a way that they knew not; I will lead them in paths that they have not known; I will make darkness light before them and crooked things straight' (Isaiah 42:16).

So, confident in this assurance, he put forward his proposal, to be met by bewildered and unbelieving eyes around the table. No 100% vote here! One concession the council did make, however, was that each member of the college staff, administrative and academic, should be asked to put in writing, without conferring with each other and after individually praying for guidance, his or her own feelings. If all were convinced that this was God's will, the council too would agree to release him.

Happy with this decision, unwilling to justify himself to the council in his conviction, but convinced that his staff would ratify what he himself felt so strongly, Stanley was content to leave the matter this way.

How easy it is, in our seeking for guidance, sometimes to get our timing wrong, even though our knowledge of His will may be right! To Stanley's astonishment, not one member of his staff felt he was in line with God's will. One even went so far as to charge him with wanting to run away from what God had given him to do, suggesting he 'settle down and get on with the job'. The nearest any came to agreeing was to assure him that although not happy about his thinking on wider ministry 'I have enough confidence in your discernment of His will for you, to stand by you in any decision you make'.

So although he was disappointed, baffled though not dismayed by the corollary of the Emmanuel executive council's decision which followed, he was not shaken and believed firmly that it would be a matter of perhaps just a few months before everyone came to see as he saw. In fact, it was four years before this happened.

Although sure of God's guidance, he had somehow mis-timed it; but, as subsequent events were to prove, God's clock is never wrong—though ours may be.

During these four years two or three serious crises developed in the college which only Stanley had the necessary knowledge to deal with, and he began to see why God had kept him at 'the job'. At the end of these years, once again the subject was broached by a fellow council member (not by Stanley himself—he was determined to wait until God opened the door): 'Do you still feel,' he asked Stanley, 'as strongly about a wider ministry as you did four years ago?'

'Yes,' he replied, 'every bit.'

And this time not only the direction but the timing too of the guidance was right, although he still had no plan for the way forward. But the Lord's plan for a new principal unfolded in the form of the Rev. Lionel Hawker and the confirmation in Stanley's heart of his will came in the shape of a letter within a month of his receiving the 'green light' from the council.

In Greenwood, Indiana, USA, a man of God had been constrained by the Holy Spirit to give himself to prayer for a week regarding a deep need in the mission of which he was president. The burden on his heart was that God would supply someone who could pastor missionaries in their overseas assignments by means of personal counselling and retreats: who would teach and encourage national pastors in third-world countries and who would conduct courses of lectures in the seminaries of these countries.

The man was Dr Wesley Duewel, and the mission was the OMS International. OMS had been founded in 1901 by Charles and Lettie Cowman, and originally was known as the Oriental Missionary Society. In its early days the mission was concentrated in Far East countries, but it is now operating too in South and Central America, Asia, Europe and West Indies, with its headquarters in USA and national headquarters in Canada, South Africa, New Zealand, Australia and Great Britain.

As Dr Duewel prayed, the Holy Spirit laid the name of Stanley Banks on his heart as one who could do this work of minister-at-large. He had known Stanley and had kept in touch with the work of Emmanuel for many years, yet had no idea of the Lord's recent leadings in Stanley's life. The more Dr Duewel prayed, the deeper was the impression on this heart that 'Stanley was the man'. Hence the letter of invitation to Stanley to join OMS landed on his desk one month after his 'release'.

It was not going to be easy to sever links—visible links, that is—with Emmanuel after well over thirty years in its close fellowship, but as the future pattern unfolded it was plain that the inner and less visible ties would not be broken; we simply gained more friends, new colleagues, wider circles and, most important of all, the knowledge of His will being fulfilled in our lives in new and untrodden ways. Perhaps it is appropriate to say that at this initial stage I was not able, for reasons of domestic ties, to join Stanley in his overseas travels, but ultimately this became possible, so our joy in serving the Lord in this way together was doubled.

The vision given to Dr Duewel during his week of prayer began to be realised. The way opened for tours, usually lasting for two or three months, to many of the OMS fields, including Korea, Japan, Hong Kong, Taiwan, Indonesia, India, Europe (Spain and France), Colombia, Ecuador and Haiti. Stanley also spent time in the countries with overseas headquarters: New Zealand, Australia, South Africa, Canada—and of course in the British Isles.

During the tours of third-world countries, the times Stanley spent with the missionaries were very precious, though often full of pressures and problems, for missionaries say emphatically, 'No haloes, please! We're human!' He spent many hours getting to grips with the kind of relationship problems you and I face, but with the added pressures of living in a different culture and climate; with the administration situations common to any work of God, but with added complications that arise because of distance from 'head office' or through breakdown in communications with nationals; with the problems arising because of local government 'red tape', or through the misguided feeling that 'our Western way' of doing things is necessarily the only way.

Sometimes it was hard to be faithful as he gave advice in a difficult situation, but one missionary spoke of being 'always encouraged and educated by his words', yet another of the 'countless spiritual boosts' he gave and the 'deep and lasting impact he made on our lives from the very first time he spoke to us and the Korean pastors and in the seminary in Seoul'. A young missionary to a new work in France spoke of the 'undergirding of our ministry and the significant help you gave Mary and me to make the best decision at an important crossroads'. During the time spent in Colombia, South America, there were some deep problems and needs to be faced buut throughout those days of sharing, praying and seeking people noticed that Stanley 'had the gift of being "a father" to many of us'. While one or another remembers 'his prayerful and personal concern', 'his penetrating ministry' or 'his wise counsel', others thank God for 'his beaming face', 'his fun in the home', 'his benevolent kindness', 'his Christian gentlemanliness', 'his friendly spirit', 'his informality' and 'his wonderful sense of humour'.

But counselling and relating to others' needs and problems was never easy for him. Often the burdens he carried in this way needed many hours of prayer and seeking for answers from God, but he was fearless in his response to the inwardness of the needs he recognised in the missionary flock for whom he had been given responsibility, and he always looked for positive results, even though such times often produced great weariness of body and mind.

Those who knew Stanley and have shared his delight in expounding God's truth will realise readily that the part of his overseas assignment that gave him the most joy and fulfilment was his ministry to the national pastors in their conferences and retreats and to the students of the seminaries. In most countries this had to be done by interpretation, and he developed a wonderful rapport with his interpreters. He would often recount stories against himself about what impossible situations his hard-worked interpreters would find themselves in, when he used obscure English clichés or colloquialisms, as when he spoke of the Holy Spirit's work being that of an 'ex*e*cutor' of God's plan in a believer's life, only to learn afterwards that his interpreter had translated the title into a word meaning '*ex*ecutor' (with the emphasis on the first syllable!).

His sessions with pastors and students not only dealt with theology, homiletics, Biblical doctrines, etc, but with many practical issues such as pastoral theology, family life and church administration. And always he allowed time for questions and personal counselling. The sessions were strenuous and took their toll on Stanley physically. On his return home from a tour, which would usually culminate in a long-haul flight and its consequent jet-lag, he would need some time to recover equilibrium and renewed strength. His favourite translation of Psalm 91:1 from the literal Arabic, and one which he quoted often was: 'He that maketh as his permanent abode the secret place of the Most High, shall always be in touch with the Almightiness of God.' At these times this 'secret abode' was his source of strength, enabling him to carry on into the next tour 'by his dynamic power'.

One of Stanley's great enjoyments in his travels was seeing and participating in other cultural activities and experiences. He always bore in mind the cliché (so well-known it was almost whiskered in missionary circles) that this or that strange custom or behaviour was 'not wrong, only different'. So when on his first visit to a Korean home he was invited to sit (or whatever the necessary position could be known as) on a cushion at a low table to partake of a long, leisurely Korean meal, he manfully endured the increasing cramp and deadness in his legs, till on trying to rise he found himself, as he put it, 'naturalised in the unnatural', and took an eternity to make one foot move after the other. Or who can forget his description of his endeavours to eat his first meal with chopsticks? 'The finest way to slim,' he would say. 'For the amount which reaches your mouth is negligible.'

He was fortunate when in Haiti that there was a dentist on the compound in Cap Haitien, for his efforts to eat the national cassava bread without the customary 'dunking' usually indulged in by the missionaries resulted in a broken dental plate! And in India, he was fortunate that there was a dish of bananas on the table at a curry (hot, hot!) dinner he shared with the students in the Madras seminary, for 'Bananas' (they informed him) 'would take the heat out of the curry.' And did they need to, for him—he who hated curry!

This Britisher could never come to terms with doughnuts or Danish pastries for breakfast in the USA, although he did come to enjoy maple syrup on his bacon. And he very quickly learned to call potato crisps by their American title of chips, a car boot a trunk, a pavement a sidewalk and a car bonnet a hood. He was nothing if not adaptable to the vast number of changes and differences that made such a noticeable part of this era of his life.

Part of Stanley's assignment was to include a tour of some of the United States, in order to make known the work of OMS and to be a back-up for furloughing missionaries on deputation tours, ministering to congregations alongside the missionaries as they challenged their hearers with the need of mission.

Perhaps this was his greatest test of stamina, which at one end of the scale involved weeks of one-night stops, living out of a suitcase, long journeys by road across the States, meeting new friends daily, being entertained royally (thus putting on many unneeded calories, however enjoyable!). But at the other end of the scale he met a lack of response to missionary challenge, had to combat materialism as he presented the need of third-world countries, stirring hearts to think outside their own comfortable environment and well-ordered church lives to appreciate the depth of concern many nationals have for their own people still in the dark, as he sought to convey to his hearers the spiritual maturity of many overseas church leaders. As Stanley himself said, after a tour in Haiti, 'I didn't feel I'd gone there to give them (the pastors) anything—I'd gone to learn from them.' And he would tell of the daily, early-morning praying by a handful of Christians in a devil-ridden village, which resulted eventually in an outpouring of God's Spirit when hundreds were brought out of darkness into light. How hard it seemed to him to impress on these Western Christians the absolutely vital importance of prayer if the powers of darkness were to be bound, whether in voodoo-ridden Haiti or in the superficial, materialistic West!

In spite of the burdens he carried deep within him, these were never allowed to cloud his fellowship or his fun in the many homes he visited. He formed lasting friendships in churches and homes over the USA.

In the last two or three years of Stanley's time with OMS he was suddenly, reluctantly and unavoidably 'grounded'. A situation arose in the British constituency which necessitated his becoming director, so his tours overseas were cancelled, to the sorrow of us both, for the challenge of overseas mission and the resultant burden and inspiration had made lasting inroads into our hearts. The position was certainly one he did not choose, and it was one which cost more to him in self-discipline (for he disliked administration), and in the leaving of a work which he had grown to love with all his heart, than he could have imagined.

A poem of Amy Wilson Carmichael's which he often prayed was the essence of his longing now, as never before, as he realised afresh that he was at the Lord's disposal, whatever that might mean for him, and however difficult it might be. It was still the dynamic power that would enable him and the love that leads the way which would constrain him:

From prayer that asks that I may be
Sheltered from winds that beat on Thee,
From fearing when I should aspire.
From faltering when I should climb higher,
From silken self, O Captain, free
Thy soldier who would follow Thee.

From subtle love of softening things,
From easy choices, weakenings,
Not thus are spirits fortified,
Not this way went the Crucified,
From all that dims Thy Calvary,
O Lamb of God, deliver me.

Give me the love that leads the way,
The faith that nothing can dismay,
The hope no disappointments tire,
The passion that will burn like fire,
Let me not sink to be a clod:
Make me Thy fuel, Flame of God.

CHAPTER 5

'NOT JUST A TEACHER...'

HIS WIDER PUBLIC and circle of acquaintances respected and valued Stanley as an able teacher of scriptural truth, but one who came within his closer circle of friends during the last few years of his life spoke of her appreciation in having had 'such a gentleman as a teacher *and a friend*'.

Whether in the small Derbyshire village of his childhood, his college days, the time spent in Scotland's glens evangelising; whether through the ordered, routine, long, rewarding and fulfilling years in Emmanuel church and college, living in close relationships; whether travelling the world on his missionary assignments with OMS visiting many homes with varying cultures; whether in his days of retirement (so-called!) in Cheshire village life, as he formed new and deep bonds in the fellowship of the church to which we were led during his last few years... wherever he was, I had always known that his capacity for friendship-forming was something unique. It permeated staff relationships, platform-sharing, church fellowship and village life.

John Turner, the lad with whom Stanley sought and found the Lord as a teenager, speaks still of him as 'his best friend', one to whom he could always tell his troubles and who always understood him. Colleagues in EBC days were not only that: they became friends, too. Forty years on, they speak of the 'privilege of being old friends of Stanley Banks' '. The rapport in church business between pastor and his secretary, Arthur, was another relationship which deepened into a life-long friendship. It began before Arthur's days as secretary to Stanley, when as a 'lone Christian in the forces, Stanley's letters of encouragement supported me; coming home on leave his welcome was genuine. His heart and his home were always open to receive me and my family. Our fellowship was rich in things pertaining to the kingdom of God'. Arthur remembers that 'many hours were spent in very profitable debate and discussion (sometimes with weary wives waiting ([im]patiently). His interests were so interestingly broad, from evangelism to evolution, from revival to politics. We all know about his preaching in the pulpit, but how many know of his stoking the old church coke-burning boiler, shovelling away like mad on a Sunday morning before going up into the pulpit to preach?'

Perhaps this was one of the indispensable ingredients of his ability to form lasting and rewarding friendships: his way of entering into the practicalities, the problems, the patent needs, and the inner hurts of his friends and colleagues. A fellow missionary in Ecuador tells me that the thing he remembers most about him is 'how totally interested he was in everything going on around him. We were on a tour to visit a remote valley church, and as we were returning up the steep road afterwards, a radiator pipe in the Land Rover burst.' (Anyone who has visited Ecuador knows the impossibility of obtaining a repair man on those remote, hazardous mountain trails; you are your own mechanic, or else!) Peter continues: 'We then proceeded to do roadside repairs, refilling the engine from a nearby stream. Stanley was totally involved in this, giving practical suggestions and help in whatever way possible. I saw from this that he did not come to Ecuador simply to preach but to be involved in every aspect of our lives.'

One whose friendship with Stanley dates back to the '40s in Emmanuel days, writes 'We were first of all friends; then he became my pastor, then when I was a student in the college, my tutor and Bible teacher... but first my friend.'

A more superficial assessment of his capacity for friendship, but none the less contributory, has been the repetitive reference to the 'smile that was ready at any moment to spread across his face and which radiated out to include whoever he was with. I was always encouraged when I met him'.

His encouragement was not the only feature of visits he made over many years to one home in Nottingham. He is remembered there not only as a 'very kind and loving man of God who helped and encouraged us in the Lord', but for 'his wonderful sense of humour'. This humorous trait was often most noticeable in his interest in the children of the homes he visited. One mother remembers that during family prayers after a meal, she 'opened her eyes to see what Barbara, eighteen months old, was up to. I need not have worried,' she adds. 'Barbara was being entertained by the principal!'

When he was in New Zealand, four children in a home where he was staying dearly loved him 'and always confided in him because he listened and responded to them. They loved to sit on his knee and have stories read to them. Often he would feed the youngest and keep them all amused on wet days. The children looked on him as "somewhere between Dad and God" who although a man of prayer was humble enough to be interested in them and their activities'.

Years later, when in our retirement we moved to the small village of Barrow, in rural Cheshire, we had no fears about whether we could adapt to a country environment and country people. Or maybe I should be more honest and say that I knew Stanley would be the advance guard in this respect. How right I was! The village church, the village bowling club, the village shop were all quickly included in his outgoing friendliness and warmth. Having lived so much of life in an institutional set-up, it was almost a novel experience to have neighbours: neighbours who quickly became friends, and who later were to speak of him as 'our kind and charming neighbour', one whom 'we always respected, love and admired'.

It is not easy to distinguish between the friend and the counsellor. Perhaps we shouldn't try to; often the friendship came out of the counselling, and even more often the long-standing friendship would shift into a counselling situation.

Because of the friendship he maintained with colleagues, it was easier for them to accept advice, counsel or even correction; the underlying love and mutual respect kept the balance. Missionaries he visited in Morocco remember that 'during a difficult time he sought to bring harmony where there was discord and gave us his wise counsel, even though it was hard to follow, and we were tempted to question it.'

His answer for a harmonious relationship was a prayerful attitude of a willingness to give as well as take. If he happened to be the minister who 'tied the knot' of their marriage, people certainly remember him saying in his brief talk in the service, 'Learn to say, "I'm sorry," and "I'm wrong." Marriages are broken up by feminine popes and masculine tyrants.'

Co-staff, co-missionaries, co-board members found it was easy to talk to Stanley and to ask his advice or opinion. 'You never felt that he was judgmental.' A missionary remembers that in a problematic situation 'he would never say, "This is what you should do." He always enabled you to open your mind to see the full picture from every angle, and then from this perspective make your own decision and see what was the best way forward.'

But anyone involved in a counselling ministry knows that advice is not always accepted or acted upon. Not infrequently, especially during his years as principal of the college, Stanley would be saddened by an unwilling attitude in a student, a spirit of rebellion and reluctance to profit from the discipline of training and relationship with others, or by headstrong waywardness. He was human enough to wonder, on such occasions, if he had given the right advice or shown enough love. Never over-confident in his own wisdom, he would sometimes need assurance and would ask me, 'Do you think I said the right thing?' or he would comment, 'I can't do any more—I'll just have to leave it in the Lord's hands.' There were times when, in faithfulness, he may have seemed hard or harsh; there were also times when his keeping silent rather than vindicating himself as he took a decision, refusing to break a confidence, produced misunderstandings. In

'NOT JUST A TEACHER...'

these situations others sometimes felt he was wrong and maybe, not being infallible, he was; but he was content to commit such things into higher hands.

In the last two years of Stanley's life the counselling developed a new slant which gave him the accolade of the Spirit's anointing. To our home in Barrow came a steady stream of mature men of God, seeking advice and prayer fellowship as they faced new decisions, mid-life crises or a desire for guidance in a changing future. He found this more a challenge and an inspiration than a means of exhibiting wisdom or experience. And as he had less physical strength for the strenuous ministry of previous years, he was encouraged as he recognised that the Lord still had a rewarding work for him to do.

CHAPTER 6

MAN AND MESSAGE

You say you do not want a eulogy, and I can understand your feeling in this. But it is difficult to avoid when I remember his godliness and steadfastness. My most vivid and lasting memory of Stanley is from the first time I heard him minister. I was struck by his Christlike countenance, an impression I kept right through our friendship, which Cyril and I valued so much. I recall, too, his sincerity: I always felt at ease in his presence, and he instilled confidence wherever he was.

S0 WROTE A FRIEND with whom we shared many wonderful times of fellowship, relaxation and fun, thereby underlining the thought expressed by one of his oldest friends who knew him better than many when she said, 'The man and the message were one'; or to put it in the words of another, 'His own personal experience of the completeness of God's salvation brought such an assured and confident ring to his witness.'

And yet this very aura of confidence and the ability to create it in those around him was something he only experienced through God's 'dynamic power'. For we who were closest to him, frequently sensed in him an apprehension and doubt of his own trust or assurance.

On one occasion when driving towards a week's discussion and lectures in a northern teacher training college, he was so full of fears of those whom he felt could easily defeat him in argument because of their supposed superior intellect that he pulled into a lay-by to talk to the Lord and quieten his spirit. He told how the Lord came to him with assurance and peace telling him, 'You don't have to defend me or win arguments—all you have to do is proclaim me.' So with a confidence beyond himself he went on the road again.

Like all of us, he had his own private fears and apprehensions. He once surprised me when he told me that he felt the familiar 'butterflies' each time before he went into the pulpit to proclaim God's word, and that after giving a message, the devil's temptation to doubt its effectiveness would often come to him. But through the years he learned more of the secret of bringing these fears and temptations to the place of strength, even though they were there to the end.

One day we talked freely to each other about our greatest natural fears, and to my surprise he brought his out without a moment's hesitation: 'Going into hospital.' In this I recognised not merely a fear of the physical problems that might be involved but something deeper which, although a very hidden thing, was none the less very poignant to him: his fear of new and untried situations. But when the day came when it was no longer just a possibility but a reality (for the first time in his life), he coped with it in the way he always did with new experiences: with outward confidence and a stabilising inner peace. At a very natural level, I always knew when he had fears as he faced something of which he was nervous or afraid, for he would softly hum to himself, nothing specific or in a minor key: just a brief, happy-sounding hum!

In preparing Stanley's story I wrote to many friends, colleagues, associates of all ilks, past and present, asking for each one's particular memory of him. So often the replies were worded much like this one from the writer of the foreword, Dr Denis Applebee, long-time colleague in Emmanuel: 'Whether we can fulfil your request that it should be neither eulogistic nor character-assessing, I doubt, for Mr Banks was to us such a character of quality that whatever we may say might fall into one of these two categories.'

One young minister commented that he had a 'compassionate spirit towards other believers.' This was always noticeable as his ministry led him to many churches and denominations across the board, with as many shades of doctrine and interpretation of truth. With his gift of 'rightly dividing the word of truth' came the presentation of it in a way that was acceptable to his hearers, even those who may have listened initially with prejudiced ears.

Dr Applebee summed up his thoughts about Stanley like this:

His Biblical setting for each truth gave him wider acceptance with each year, and this became the hallmark of his life's ministry. Having followed in his footsteps from time to time in other parts of the world, I have heard this comment over and over again. His presentation was one hundred per cent scriptural. This broke down the walls of prejudice and opened minds to see that wonderful inheritance God has for every believer. The work of the Holy Spirit was presented in such scriptural terms that every message was Christ-centred and Christ-revealing, unveiling some new aspect of his person and ministry within the believer. When, after years of leadership, the time came when he felt called to a wider, freer mnistry, it was difficult for some of us to accept his going. He quietly slipped out of the harness into the next chapter of God's work without the slightest desire to be remembered or memorialised. But those who came under his teaching cannot forget the truths imparted, for the pen may have been human, but the ink was of the Spirit, indelibly written upon our lives through a man who walked quietly into and out of them, making our own transitions easier by example.

'I am not called to be an evangelist,' Stanley would say. 'God has not given me the gift of evangelism. He has called me to be a teacher of His Word.' And although, as was so often the case, the 'evangel' was faithfully and clearly proclaimed within the scope of his ministry, yet his gift was always most noticeable and predominant in the field of teaching. And although he felt himself to be ungifted in writing, over the years he published several small books containing series of lectures, talks or messages which had already been given in churches, conventions and colleges. While at Emmanuel Bible College he compiled and printed the entire Bible study course for his students. In all his research into the background and origin of Scripture—its history, text and teaching—he drew extensively on such scholars as the Rev. Sidlow Baxter, Dr A.T. Pierson, the Rev. J. Brice and others; but John Wesley's heritage for him was the kingpin of much of his study of Bible doctrine.

Before every message he gave, he disciplined himself to intensive study and preparation of mind, as well as warming his own heart and challenging his own emotions and will by the subject matter on hand. He rarely, if ever, preached with notes, for he would almost invariably write out in full the message he was to give. Digressions during the preaching were almost nil. When young folk came to him, questioning him about study and preparation, suggesting that this did not leave scope for the Spirit's inspiration during preaching, they would quote to him, 'Open thy mouth wide and I will fill it.'

'Then,' he would say, 'the Lord gets the blame for the rubbish that comes out.'

He never had time for a sermon which was a connected (or unconnected) string of stories and illustrations, for to him it was important that there should be real 'meat' and not just 'desserts' in his presentation of truth. However, he was remembered by many for his apt illustrations, some of which he gleaned from the writings of E. Stanley Jones and from F.W. Boreham's *Great Text Series*. He always believed it was important to the theme of his message to make a point clear by illustration, and even, on occasions, to wake up his hearers by this exercise. But more often his illustrations came from his own experience of family life, travel, people and of simple observation of the world around him.

He loved to emphasise the importance of demonstrating the Christian life as well as preaching about it by telling of the tremendous change in his parents' life during his own teenage years: of the fresh impetus, the new interests, the kindly love and tolerance entering the home, which impressed his young mind and heart.

'Friends,' he would say, 'it was not a sermon that brought me to Christ! It was the transformation in my parents' lives that gave me a hunger to know Christ for myself.'

From his mid-teen years, working as an electrical engineering student in the Derbyshire coalmine, he would illustrate the constant cleansing possible in the life of the believer, by asking, 'Can you tell me what part of a miner's body never gets black? He is black from head to foot when he comes up the shaft and has to shower before he goes home. But there is one part of him which never gets dirty. What is it?' After waiting (usually in vain) for an answer, he gave the solution to the riddle. 'It's the white of his eye! Why? Because the lachrymal gland produces a fluid which flows constantly over the eye and keeps it clean and free from pollution.'

Speaking of the function of the Holy Spirit to make actual in our lives what the Lord Jesus did for us at Calvary, he told of the night on Liverpool Pier Head when speaking at an open air meeting. A heckler called out, 'How can what a man did 2,000 years ago possibly affect me today?'

'I'm the Executor of a man's will,' Stanley began. 'While he is alive I have nothing to do, but as soon as he dies I am responsible for the distribution of his wealth in exactly the way he has willed it. His wealth is not mine; I can't use it for myself; I can't spend it; I can't give it to whom I like. I'm responsible to make available to his legatees just what he has willed. So the Holy Spirit's work, as Jesus' Executor, is to make real to me and available for me all that Jesus did for me on Calvary.'

To press home his insistence that the Holy Spirit wants us to co-operate with him, he would tell the delightful story of what happened in a Scottish Highland village during a service he attended. The organ was of rather ancient vintage, of the kind that has its wind pumped into it by an organ blower (usually a young boy) at its back, while the organist draws on his strenuous efforts by playing the hymns for the congregation.

'On this occasion,' Stanley recounted, 'the sermon was rather long and dreary. The preacher gave out the closing hymn, to the relief of the congregation. The organist took his seat at the organ, put his hands on the keyboard, but not a tweet came out of it. After a moment's awkward silence, he slipped off his seat and went round to the back of the organ...to wake up the organ blower. The playing,' he finished with great pointedness, 'had to be a joint effort; no organ blowing, no music.'

Very many of his illustrations came from our family life. He would speak of the delight the Lord has in his children's love by telling of a Sunday morning when he was closeted in his study, preparing and praying about his sermon for the morning service. A faint tap at the door was followed by the appearance of our four-year old son.

'Daddy, can I come in?'

'Not at the moment, son; Daddy's very busy.'

But despite this rejoinder, the boy was undaunted. He climbed on Daddy's knee and flung two chubby arms around his neck, exclaiming, 'I just wanted to say, "I love you, Daddy."'

On a less tender occasion, there were recriminations following quite a serious misdemeanour. But Daddy felt considerably deflated when the same son reproachfully bellowed out loudly, 'But, Daddy, something inside me made me do it.' How clear an illustration this gave him of the in-dwelling power of original sin and of how much under Satan's power we all are, apart from the grace of God!

Many will remember the quite amazingly appropriate illustration he used when speaking of the measure of the Holy Spirit's possession of the believer and the degree of filling possible:

> As a family, for several years, we rented a holiday cottage at the north of the island of Skye in the Hebrides. We booked it the first year without seeing it, so on arrival we were all keen to see what we had rented. After the younger generation had made a hasty dash round the house, downstairs and then upstairs, the voice of our younger daughter came from above. 'Hey, there's a room up here that's locked. See if you can find a key, Dad.'
>
> But there was no key to be found.
>
> 'See if there's a ladder in the shed so that we can look in from the outside.'
>
> But there was no ladder.
>
> 'Look, Dad, stand under the window and I'll stand on your shoulders. Then I can see in.'
>
> So, like an obedient father, I stood where I was told; she climbed on my shoulders and looked through the window.
>
> 'Wow,' she shouted, 'it's just full of junk!'
>
> So although we had been given the key to the house, we did not have full possession of it. There was a room full of junk which the owner did not want us to see. Have you a junk room in your life, full of things you don't want to hand over to God?

He also made use of a minor family dispute to illustrate the assurance and safety which we can know in our lives if we allow the Lord to be our File-leader, our Forerunner, the Author and Finisher of our faith:

> Our elder son spent some time working with VSO (Voluntary Service Overseas) in Kenya and while there

acquired a love for rock climbing. So on his return, replete with all things necessary, he began to work on our younger daughter, aged fourteen, who was always game for anything active, as well as being fearless. So one Saturday morning, he came downstairs with climbing kit and ropes, followed by his sister, also suitably rigged out.
'Oh, no, you don't!' said her mother. 'It's much too dangerous.'
'Oh, please, Mum,' pleaded the aspiring climber.
'Listen, Mother,' interposed Ian. 'Meryl will be quite safe. She will always be roped to me, and I'll always be in the lead.'

At the end of such a story, little explanation was needed. Listeners got the point!

One of Stanley's favourite experiences and one which he loved to talk about was drawn from his first visit to South Africa. It illustrated what a difference Christ makes in a life and proves that no matter how much of this world's wealth and fame we may have, we are still empty without Christ; it also shows how important it is that we preach a sermon with our lives.

He had received six months' leave of absence from the college while he was still principal, and during the time in South Africa spent a week conducting a series of meetings in the docks mission at Gleemore in the Cape Province. It was a series for believers rather than an evangelistic outreach. One night as he looked out from the platform over the large coloured congregation, he noticed one white face, the only one there apart from his own. At the end of the service, during the last hymn, the leader whispered to Stanley, 'I feel strongly led to make an appeal to any who may not know the Lord.'

Stanley takes up the story:

About eight people responded to the appeal, among them this very smartly dressed white lady.

'I think you'd better pray with her, Stanley,' said the leader. 'She mightn't approve of one of us.'

So I took her into the vestry and had the unspeakable joy of leading her to Christ. Then my curiosity got the better of me, and I asked her, 'What brought you here, to this coloured* church, tonight?' I had noticed she seemed ill at ease, didn't appear to know the hymns and had no Bible with her (in a church where *everyone* brought a Bible).

Then she told me, 'I am married to a very successful business man; we have a beautiful home and a lovely family. We employ several coloured* servants. One of them comes to this church and always goes about her work singing. She is paid a low wage, has nothing of the wealth and luxury that I have and yet she's always happy and smiling. I've watched her for a long time, asking myself why I, who have everything, am unhappy, while she, who has nothing and works hard all the time for the little she gets, is always happy. So this morning, I called her to me and asked her the reason. 'It's quite simple, Madam,' she replied. 'I have Jesus and you don't!'

And then with a stroke of genius she added, 'Madam, we have an Englishman preaching at our church tonight. Why don't you come and hear him?'

'So,' she said, 'that is why I'm here. I want to know Jesus like my little servant.'

So it wasn't my sermon that brought her to Christ, but the shining of a little servant girl in whom Christ dwelt.

---

* The mixed races of South Africa are classified as 'Coloureds'.

From his early days in EBC Stanley's ministry quickly began to extend beyond the confines of the local church and college. His early allegiance to and love for the JEB brought an invitation to him to join the board of this mission and for many years he felt very privileged to be part of it. He knew that although the door to Japan had closed for him, he could still help to carry the burden of such a needy land. He enjoyed wonderful fellowship with members of the band, speaking often at their conventions at Swanwick and elsewhere.

Opportunities for ministry at other conventions grew through the years, including the League of Prayer, Faith Mission (Edinburgh) conventions in Scotland, England and Ireland. The latter he particularly appreciated because of his past association with the mission: Ireland and its people became especially dear to him. He shared ministry at the Gideons International convention and, although never taking more than a listener's part of the Keswick Convention, he spoke at many local 'Keswick' conventions, not only in Britain, but also in New Zealand and Hong Kong. For a number of successive years he was very much part of the Southport International Revival Convention, where memories of the house-parties he led are alive with the joy and fellowship shared.

But of all the opportunities for service and ministry outside his work in EBC and OMS perhaps the one that gave him the greatest fulfilment was in the later years of his life, when he was invited to record messages of foundational Christian truths in basic English for broadcasting to the West Coast of Africa (through ELWA radio station). To feel he was reaching out through radio to some in the third world, even after his travels to them had stopped, was a great compensation.

Man and Message

He did several series, but the one which brought the most response was entitled *Portraits of Christ*, the first study of which I quote in full, to complete the picture of the man and his message:

> It is many centuries since Christ was born in Bethlehem and lived for over thirty years in Palestine, before being crucified by the Romans at the request of the Jewish authorities.
>
> Since those days many artists have painted pictures of Christ, and many statues of him have been made and placed in churches and public places, but none of the people who painted the pictures or made the statues had ever seen him. Their work was just the product of their imagination, what they thought he was like.
>
> But we do have an account of his life and work, and of the kind of person he was, written by four different writers who had either lived and worked with him or had direct contact with those who had. Their writings have been preserved for us in the four gospels with which the New Testament of the Bible begins. It is with these that we shall begin this series of studies. Then we will go on to look at some of the names which were given to Christ, and some which he used himself to describe his ministry while here on earth.
>
> In the four gospels there are four separate portraits of Christ. Each of the four writers gives his own impression of the life, character and work of the Lord, and of the things he taught. Each of them was writing for a different group of people, and so presented Christ in a way that their readers would understand and appreciate.
>
> Matthew, being an orthodox Jew, wrote his gospel particularly for Jewish readers. He records those things in the life and teaching of the Lord Jesus which would be of interest to a Jew. He is seeking to show his readers that Christ is the Messiah of whom the Jewish prophets of the Old Testament of the Bible spoke and that he was a

descendant of the famous Jewish king, David. He sees Christ as the King and presents him as such, including in his writings all those things which reveal Christ's authority. He presents his readers with Christ's teaching on the kingdom of God of which Christ is king.

Mark's picture of Christ is quite different. He writes to interest readers from among the Romans, and he has in mind the non-Jewish sections of the population. The thing that impresses Mark when he thinks of the life of Christ is that he is servant of all, always seeking to meet the needs of those around him. He does not expect them to serve him because he has come to serve them. On one occasion when his disciples were seeking positions of power and prominence in his coming kingdom, Christ said to them: 'Whoever wants to become great among you must be your servant, and whoever wants to be first must be the servant of all.' He then went on to say to them: 'Even the Son of Man did not come to be served but to serve, and to give his life a ransom for many.' So, to Mark, Christ was the ideal servant.

Luke was a doctor, so it is not surprising that when he wrote his life of Christ, he looked at it through the eyes of a doctor, and he saw Christ as truly human, one who showed compassion and concern for people, healing their diseases, sharing in their sorrows, saving them from their sins, lifting up those who had fallen, receiving the outcasts and seeking the lost. Luke was also writing for Greek-speaking readers, and the Greeks were constantly looking for the 'perfect man'. Thus he is presenting Christ to his readers as the ideal man, in whom is no sin, and whose life was one of love and concern for humanity. To Luke, Christ was the Perfect Man and an example of what true humanity should be.

The last of the writers was John. When he wrote his gospel he was an old man coming to the end of his life; all the other apostles were already dead. John is writing particularly for the Christian church. His gospel is very different from the others, because he does not set out to write a life of Christ. He tells us quite clearly what his purpose was; it is stated in chapter 20, verse 31: 'These [things] are written that you might believe that Jesus is the Christ, the Son of God, and that believing you might have life through his name.' He is telling his readers that he had a twofold purpose in writing: it was to record those events which showed that Jesus was the Son of God, and also to inform his readers about eternal life, which can be received only through Christ. As the Son of God, Christ has come to bear away the sin of the world and to bring mankind eternal life. John's gospel is perhaps the most loved and most read of all the four, because it shows us who Christ is and why he came into the world.

So these are the four gospels with their four separate portraits of Christ, but when taken together they provide us with a unique picture of his life and work and of his character. We shall look at each of these portraits in the next four talks and see what we can learn about the Lord Jesus Christ and what he demands of us.

CHAPTER 7

TO THE UTTERMOST PARTS...

THE 1961 TOUR OF South Africa and Swaziland was a great adventure for Stanley. It was his first opportunity to reach those 'uttermost parts' which (as far as he was concerned) were included in his Master's commission. And during those months the seeds were sown in his heart in preparation for the wider ministry that would eventually open up to him.

Throughout his life, Stanley kept no diaries, but he did write an extensive and exhaustive account of his tour of South Africa, recording his observations, impressions and reactions to what he saw and experienced. Much of his time there was spent with the Africa Evangelistic Band, a sister-mission of Scotland's Faith Mission. In Swaziland he ministered in the churches and the college of the Stegi Church of the Nazarene, where he was greatly challenged as he saw a demon-possessed woman wonderfully delivered and saved. He visited ten colleges through the whole period, including those for Africans, for coloureds and for whites, as well as many churches and camps belonging to the Baptist Church. He spoke 243 times, ministering in 44 separate churches and conventions. Was this a pre-cursor of the intensive ministry which would develop in the coming years? A deep love for South Africa and her peoples never dimmed in his heart, but the coloured people with their spirituality, devotion, evangelistic fervour and intense hunger for God, for ever held the prime place and never ceased to challenge and refresh him. On his subsequent three visits to South Africa, the times spent with the coloured people of Cape Town were highlights.

So the decade of the 70s opened the extent of Stanley's ministry still further. In going through his records I have been surprised that although he kept no diaries, there are detailed statistics of every place, college, convention or church in which he ministered throughout his more than 50 years of service: over 730 worldwide, including 50 spread over 13 states in North America, 78 in Northern Ireland and 431 in the rest of Great Britain. In addition to these statistics he recorded the subject of each message given and where it was given over all 50 years. Stanley had a very ordered and definitive mind, so this trend in his records should be no surprise!

'God gave me a wonderful bonus in my travels,' he once said. 'The variety and beauty of his handiwork in every country I've visited is a constant delight and amazement to me.' He had a glowing appreciation of the wonders of the natural world around him, and always found them a calming influence and healing balm to his spirit, whether he was among the soaring, snow-capped peaks of the Alps, where he enjoyed opening the Scriptures in WEC (Worldwide Evangelisation Crusade) holiday conferences, watching the sunsets beyond the Outer Hebrides, walking beside the River Wharfe in the Yorkshire Dales or marvelling at

Stanley Banks 'First My Friend'

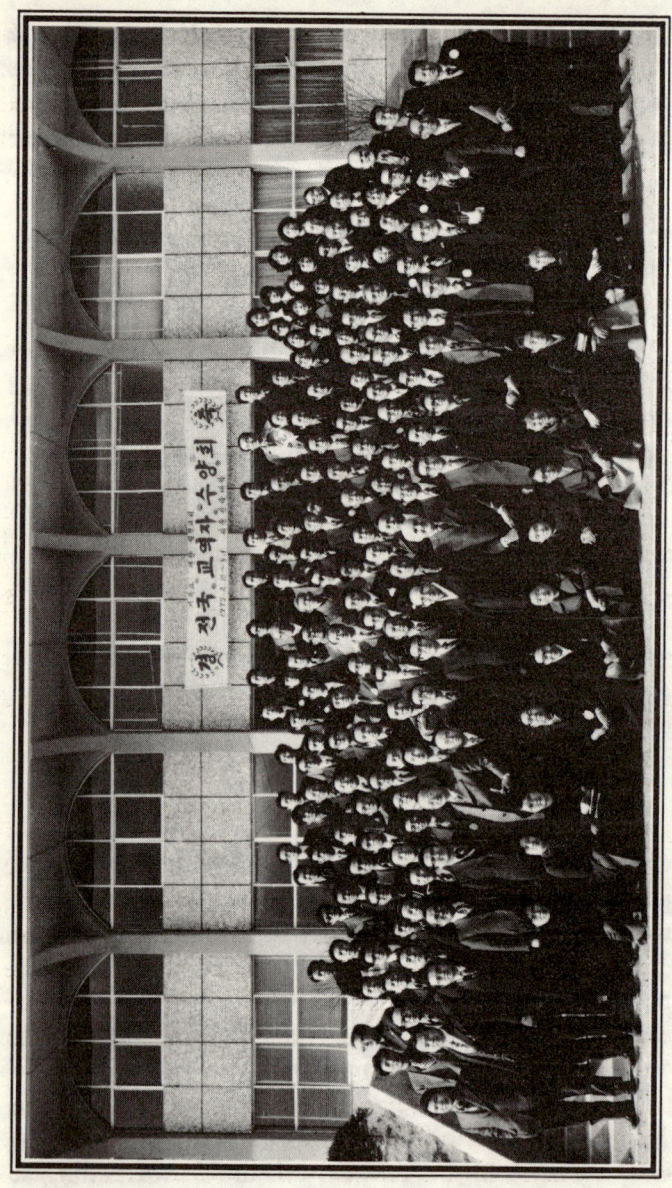

Korean Pastors' Conference, 1975 (Stanley standing centre front).

the spectacular Australian coastline of Victoria. Travelling the Garden Route by bus in South Africa presented days of quiet enjoyment, as he journeyed through dark forests and along golden shores and still lagoons, every sight bringing renewal and cause for praise.

Of the Cape Peninsula he wrote:

> For sheer physical beauty I gave it my vote: mountains, profuse flowering shrubs, delightful beaches and a paradise of fruit. The bathing at Fishoek, the beauties of the Kirstenbosch Gardens, the lights of Cape Town at night from Signal Hill are never to be forgotten experiences. So was the journey by train from Cape Town to Bloemfontein, as it slowly climbed over a mountain range at sunset, when the golden glory of this was breathtaking. I will never forget Igoda, where the Baptist Youth Camp was held, nesting in a beautifully quiet hollow away from civilisation, where mountain, river and sea meet: or a climb to the top of the mountain in the grey dawn of Easter Sunday to watch the sun rise as we sang 'Christ the Lord is risen today. Hallelujah!'

Of all the countries he visited, New Zealand was the one he most loved. Could we ever lose the beauty of the inlets and fjords of Queen Charlotte Sound as we crossed to Picton in the South Island: the surprising wonder of the geyser at Rotorua, or the unspoilt, calm beaches on the Coromandel Peninsula where we watched stilts and Caspian terns feeding their young at such close quarters that we could almost have reached out and touched them?

His capacity to enjoy each experience was so much a part of Stanley that life was made completely rewarding at every level. He was always able to relax instantly in a break for leisure, and when on holiday it did not take many days for him to unwind before he found any benefit. He had the ability to leave behind him the burdens of his work and the problems still unsolved. This applied, too, to his sleep patterns; thirty seconds after lying down he was away! In these ways his holidays and his nights were all that they ought to be in refreshment and renewal.

And what more wonderful union of beauty in a garden and assurance of the presence of a crucified yet risen Christ could be found than at the Garden tomb in Jerusalem? In 1987 Stanley was asked to lead a group to the Holy Land, a place he had never expressed any desire to visit, for he was afraid he would be disappointed by the rather blatant commercialisation of such a sacred spot. But the blessing he received and the almost overwhelming awareness that he walked where Jesus walked, and crossed the lake which Jesus calmed, was so rich that in the three years still left to him he continually referred to it in conversation and ministry.

An added joy to him in Israel came in the shape of his eldest grandchild, Timothy, who was at that time working in Jaffa among Messianic Jews. And when Timothy joined us in the house party Stanley's pride in him was radiant.

Stanley always relished travel of every kind, although he commented on more than one occasion that 'there was no glamour in hanging around an airport in the small hours of a morning, or in hours waiting for a delayed flight'; the earlier novelty of it had long worn off! And yet at the end of a long-haul flight home, his delight and excitement at returning to his home was not only because it signalled the end of yet another separation from loved ones and friends, but because he returned full of praise and humbled by the privilege that yet again he had been chosen to be his Master's messenger. He came with many stories to tell, causes for praise and challenges that had moved his own heart yet again and which he was eager to bring to others, whether it was of the teeming multitudes of India, the materialistic, self-satisfied middle classes of the Western world, the rapidly growing churches of Haiti and Latin America, or the sight of the many gripped by the thraldom and fear of false religion.

CHAPTER 8

JOY OF LIFE AND FAMILY

'DO YOU REMEMBER...?' has been one of the most frequently asked questions in letters and tributes to Stanley's life. Frequently I do remember, but many recollections—humorous, serious, poignant—have jogged my memory to no avail: others recall what I have forgotten. A few common threads are woven through many of them: his enthusiasm for living, his endearing humanity and his enjoyment of friends and family, as well as his determination not to isolate the spiritual from the natural or secular. To him, all life was one. It was permeated with gratitude to the One who had given him 'all things richly to enjoy'.

He had a life-long appreciation of poetry and good hymnology. He would illustrate God's unfailing, seeking love from his knowledge of Masefield's 'Everlasting Mercy' or from Francis Thompson's 'Hound of Heaven': he dwelt often in the thought of

>...those strong feet that followed, followed after.
> But with unhurrying chase
> And unperturbéd pace,
> Deliberate speed, majestic instancy,
> They beat—and a Voice beat
> More instant than the Feet—
> 'All things betray thee, who betrayest Me.'

F.W.H. Myers' 'St Paul' never ceased to challenge him about his attitude to the spiritually lost around him, and he would quote: 'Give me a grace upon the faint endeavour, Souls for my hire and Pentecost today.' Amy Wilson Carmichael exerted a warm influence over him in her ability to translate profound spiritual truths into verse, and in many crises and times of perplexity we would find solace together in her poem 'A Quiet Mind':

What room is there for troubled fear?
I know my Lord, and he is near;
And he will light my candle, so
That I may see the way to go.

There need be no bewilderment
To one who goes where he is sent;
The trackless plain by night and day
Is set with signs, lest he should stray.

My path may cross a waste of sea,
But that need never frighten me;
Or rivers full to very brim,
But they are open ways to him.

My path may lead through woods at night,
Where neither moon nor any light
Of guiding star or beacon shines;
He will not let me miss my signs.

Lord, grant to me a quiet mind,
That trusting thee, for thou art kind,
I may go on without a fear,
For thou, my Lord, are always near.

How often did his listeners hear him quote Wesley's hymns! Did he ever preach a sermon without giving a glimpse of the Methodist heritage of hymns of light and truth? He couldn't even start his married life without one, for we sang at our wedding service:

> Thou God of truth and love,
> We seek thy perfect way,
> Ready thy choice to approve,
> Thy providence to obey:
> Enter into thy wise design,
> And sweetly lose our will in thine.
>
> Dost thou not make us one,
> That we might one remain,
> Together travel on,
> And bear each other's pain;
> Till both thy utmost goodness prove,
> And rise renewed in perfect love?
>
> Surely thou dost unite
> Our kindred spirits here,
> That both hereafter might
> Before thy throne appear;
> Meet at the marriage of the Lamb
> And both thy glorious love proclaim.

(The slight alterations were Stanley's own!)

And so throughout his life his Wesleyan upbringing rang through his ministry as he triumphantly quoted (he loved to sing heartily—and he did, with all his might and voice):

> My trespass was gone up to heaven
> But far above the skies,
> In Christ abundantly forgiven
> I see thy mercies rise.

or of his Saviour:

> In want, my plentiful supply;
> In weakness, mine almighty power;
> In bonds, my perfect liberty;
> My light in Satan's darkest hour;
> My help and stay whene'er I call;
> In life, in death, my heaven, my all.

When explaining the incarnation how often he used the lines: 'Our God contracted to a span, Incomprehensibly made man.' He expressed the joy of his freedom from bondage and condemnation in the words from perhaps the most famous of Charles Wesley's hymns:

> Long my imprisoned spirit lay
> Fast bound in sin and nature's night;
> Thine eye diffused a quickening ray,
> I woke, the dungeon flamed with light;
> My chains fell off, my heart was free;
> I rose, went forth and followed thee.
>
> No condemnation now I dread;
> Jesus and all in him is mine;
> Alive in him, my living Head,
> And clothed in righteousness divine,
> Bold I approach the eternal throne,
> And claim the crown, through Christ, my own.

'Enlarge, inflame and fill my heart with boundless charity divine,' was a regular prayer from his heart.

Thomas Binney's 'Eternal Light' and Philip Bliss's 'Man of Sorrows' were hymns he often quoted. The last verse of Charles Wesley's 'Jesus, the name high over all' was one he always sang with the deepest desire of his heart, and its request was almost literally granted to him:

> Happy if with my latest breath
> I might but gasp his name,
> Preach him to all, and cry in death:
> 'Behold, behold the Lamb.'

———— ◇ ————

'Sounds like a giant snoring!'

So was Stanley's verdict when I first introduced him to classical music in the form of Mendelssohn's *Fingal's Cave Overture*. Brass bands and male voice choirs had been his first love, and in the early days of our relationship he just didn't want to know about any other kind of music, so we effected a workable compromise and built up a stock of 78s of both hues for our old HMV portable. But in time, almost reluctantly, we each began to appreciate one another's tastes. And although Stanley never played a musical instrument, his keen, growing ability to assess the prowess of others' musicianship was a measure of his determination to enjoy a performance. On the rare and irregular occasions when we were able to go to a concert, his enthusiasm and enjoyment were infectious. Listening to music was one of his rewarding experiences, with 'listening' being the operative word. He couldn't bear 'background' music of any kind, least of all the cacophonic beat and crash of his two teenage sons practising with their 'group' in the upper regions of home, but with whom he showed

Joy of Life and Family

an amazing tolerance—and that is more than can be said of their mother! To him, listening was an art in itself and was done with concentration, with the ear of the critic and often with eyes closed, totally relaxed.

'He was not averse to joining us in a game of football or to enquiring if we knew the latest cricket test score.' So wrote one of Stanley's ex-students, epitomising his interest in every form of sport, not only in Britain but when he visited the USA. How rapidly he began to understand the intricacies of the American sports scene! And how quickly were the roles reversed when he was able to enthuse an American colleague by his own involvement in cricket! One of them thought that the most revealing times of his friendship with Stanley were—

> when we had the pleasure of staying with you on trips to England. Here was a man, steeped in the word of God, a giant in the pulpit, living simply, loving his home and its attendant duties and getting inordinately excited over cricket test matches on the telly! 'Ed, you need to understand this marvellous sport. American baseball has nothing to compare with it,' and then he'd patiently explain what was going on—even to extolling why the match must stop for tea in mid-afternoon! You see, Stanley was a man for whom the grace of God touched the everyday things of life, which was to be enjoyed, not endured.'

His oldest granddaughter recalls 'spectating a game of cricket with him in Birkenhead Park one afternoon. His enthusiasm and enjoyment of the game was infectious. I remember too watching him playing bowls on the Barrow bowling green with friends from the village. I felt so proud that someone who could talk so convincingly about deep, highly intellectual theological issues could still relate so perfectly to people who shared so little of his first love in life.'

The Lord blessed Stanley and me with four healthy, happy children: Rachel Anne was born in April 1944, Ian Drysdale (after his maternal grandfather) in August 1945, Stuart Salway (after his paternal greatgrandfather) in March 1948 and Meryl Elizabeth in March 1953. All four were born during our time in Emmanuel Bible College, not the easiest environment in which to bring up children, but one which we know left a deep impression on their lives as they watched other young people committing themselves fully to the service of God. And of course, what children wouldn't enjoy the marvellous facility of a large garden, plenty of room to run, to play, to hide: our neighbouring children, who were their friends, far preferred our garden to their own and on occasions the scene resembled a school playground!

Between the four of them, our children gave us nine grandchildren, the ninth born the year following Stanley's homecall. Two of our children followed the Lord's calling to overseas service for a period, but all are now in Britain.

Stanley was in his element on church and family holidays and when leading youth camps. They were times of strenuous and often hilarious fun. One of his early campers from the '40s remembers him 'diving into the stream in borrowed swimming trunks to retrieve someone's shoe'. On a never-to-be-forgotten church holiday in Felixstowe, Stanley watched with amusement someone who had always swum nervously in the shallows at the beach. Suddenly he began diving repeatedly in deeper water, and Stanley thought that confidence in the sea had at last arrived. Then, suspecting that the diving was unusually prolonged, he decided to swim out to investigate, only to discover that it was not so much a desire to perfect his diving technique that was absorbing his friend as an obsession to recover his dentures, with which he had parted company as he swam. How Stanley loved to recount this story; not only that all their combined efforts were in vain, but its wonderful sequel at the next year's holiday at the same resort, when on our first expedition to the shore, the beach patrol man, recognising us from the previous year, produced for our identification a certain item of dental flotsam!

Family holidays were always special times to him, and indeed to all of us as his family, for he was never happier or more relaxed than when with us all, climbing, swimming, picnicking, exploring, beachcombing, canoeing. Saturday afternoon, too, he gave to the children. Ian recalls the winter walks, his fondest memory of his Dad:

> One of two directions was taken, either up the hill and across the golf links to watch the rugby match in Noctorum Lane, or down the hill to the New Park to stand on a mound and look over into Birkenhead Park rugby ground to watch their match. I say 'watch' with reservations; I was not tall enough to see! So up-the-hill walks were my favourites. He was always very vocal when watching a match, with instructions volunteered from the side lines, along with all the other spectators. He always had interesting comments to make and things to point out as we walked, and I feel that he was completely himself on these occasions, the father I enjoyed being with most.

Stanley and Rhoda with granddaughter Esther in USA (1974).

The other children too have referred with affection to those Saturday afternoon walks and to the holidays 'when Daddy was so relaxed and so much fun to have around; when he always had a few sweets or an apple in his pocket for a treat; we loved the Christmas treasure hunts he devised all over the college, the tennis practice in the long summer evenings on the big lawn'.

'But perhaps for me,' his older daughter, Rachel, recalls, 'my most special time was after I had gone to London to nurse and Daddy used to come up to JEB council meetings and if possible to fit in with my off-duty from Great Ormond Street Children's Hospital. He used to meet me for a cup of coffee. I know,' she concludes, 'that these are very ordinary memories, but at heart Daddy was a very ordinary person to us as children. He was just "Daddy", not a well-known preacher—just "Daddy". I hope that those who read about him will find, in the reading, both the man of God and the human person God made him.'

Stuart, his younger son, also recalling the walks over the Golf links, thinks of the kissing gate, 'through which we passed, as a kind of Narnian lamppost. It was special because he was so special and this was *our* time with him.' Stuart also recalls 'his total absorption in the Saturday afternoon school rugby games—it was only his body that wasn't actually out there playing with them! There was such a feeling of great safety when he was around; the feeling that although he wasn't there half as much as we or he wanted, yet he was totally dependable. In short, no one ever had a father of whom it was easier to feel proud than did we four. Dad made it easier to call God "Father".'

A granddaughter remembers him with—

> thoughts of great love and pride. In every way Grandad was to me the perfect grandfather...always having a welcoming smile for me, a big hand to hold, a lap to sit on and time to be interested in me individually. I was never in doubt that in some small way Grandad was proud of me, which I felt to be an immense privilege. Growing in my faith as a teenager, my love and respect for Grandad deepened as I learned from his faith, not only from hearing his preaching but also observing him practising what he preached. I am grateful to God for allowing me the privilege of sharing in just some of his life.

On the one and only wreath placed on Stanley's grave when his spirit had flown was a large card on which every member of his family (down to the youngest— our four-year-old granddaughter) had written a name

Stanley Banks 'First My Friend'

The family in 1982. Left to Right, Stuart, Rachel, Rhoda, Meryl, Stanley, Ian.

Six of Stanley and Rhoda's nine grandchildren in 1982.

JOY OF LIFE AND FAMILY

Family group, 1986. Stanley and Rhoda with daughter Meryl and granddaughters Frances and Rebecca.

Stanley and Rhoda with three grandchildren, Esther, Andrew and Jaimie (1989).

and an expression of love. One of the children wrote briefly: 'Just my Dad'.

'Who was my father?' wrote our younger daughter, Meryl.

> Was he the man who preached hundreds of sermons to thousands of people? who proclaimed the Gospel of Christ from continent to continent? who expounded the conundrums of the Christian faith with clarity and fearlessness?
>
> No, not for me.
>
> For me he was the man who demonstrated his faith by his silence, and his love by standing on Saturday mornings on a damp and windswept sports ground, supporting the school lacrosse team; who gave up his chance to sit by the fire at the end of a long day to play endless games of table tennis; who took me out on Saturday afternoons to the local rugby, cricket or football grounds—always via the sweet shop.
>
> The same man who devoted his entire adult life to God's work was also a man who had enough wisdom never to mention God to his teenage daughter, never to betray my confidence or our friendship by using our times together as an opportunity to evangelise! This unbroken trust and our common love of sport bonded us together. And now, many years later, I look back to those days and see in this unfettered companionship the seeds of my own faith.

Stuart spoke to me of the 'abiding aroma of a warm and holy life, lived for us, lived for you and lived for Jesus.'

And it was because his life was lived for Jesus that he was able to live it so fully for me, too. Perhaps the verse of Scripture which God gave us at the beginning of our life together is the best commentary on this: 'I will give them one heart and one way' (Jeremiah 32:39). So when we stood side by side in our loyalty to the work God gave us to do in Emmanuel, OMS and then (latterly) in Waverton, in our loyalty to each other in the face of criticisms or accusations, God made us one. In the way Stanley always helped in the care of our children, giving himself to their fun, friendship and spiritual needs, as well as changing nappies or mending broken toys and hearts; rambling, playing, laughing with them; or in the ability to share any household chore when there was a need of an extra pair of hands for a tea towel, or a crying babe to push to sleep or into the park—he himself made his cementing contribution to this one-ness. And through our journey together, often joyful, sometimes 'through woods at night', or 'across a waste of sea', we have claimed and seen the fulfilment of our promise. At the end we could still sing together, as we sang on our marriage day:

> Dost Thou not make us one that we might one remain,
> Together travel on and bear each other's pain?

CHAPTER 9

THE LAST LAP

ON NOVEMBER 8TH 1983, his 66th birthday, Stanley retired from OMS and its British directorship, but by no means put his feet up. Among others, I wondered how ever he had found time to direct when I watched his diary filling up more than ever before. He was freer now to take appointments for ministry and counselling than he had been through the past years.

Two premises he had always stood upon, and now in retirement as much as ever: firstly, that he would never seek to go anywhere uninvited or push open doors of ministry with his own hand; and secondly, that, if free, he would go to minister God's word wherever he was asked. And, surprise, surprise, this opened an ever widening sphere in retirement. There was almost no denomination in which he had not shared the truths of God, sometimes without a repeat invitation and, let it be said, occasionally hardly wishing for one!

In the days of retirement it was a warming and spiritually exhilarating experience for us to be together in this freer ministry, often returning to fellowships and friends of long-standing, but also meeting and making many new ones and forging lasting friendships.

'I think these are the best days of our life,' Stanley said to me as we walked one day through the Wirral Way. I knew what he meant; it was as much the delight of using a free hour revelling in the lanes and coasts of our home peninsula of Wirral as it was or ever had been 'working together with him' in a long life of service, often governed by the clock. A picnic by the Dee Estuary bird-watching, a clamber up the slopes of North Wales' Moel Fammau, a quick fifteen-minute constitutional through the old kissing gate and over the golf links or a brisk walk round the West Kirby Marine Lake—these were joys for which there had been little time in previous years. Time now, too, to linger over our personal and joint devotions, always important, but now richer and unhurried. And how he sated his mind and heart in longer hours of study of God's word!

And then came the beginning, as gradually and softly as an autumn sunrise, of our love-affair with a young and growing fellowship in a Cheshire village called Waverton.

And an invitation to preach in a barn had to be a *first!* But did we guess where this would lead?

After months of prayer for guidance, a small group of Christians anxious to establish an evangelical witness in their village cleared out a surplus barn, carpet-stripped the floor, found a piano, some stackable chairs, lots of enthusiasm and hunger for God's word and a burden for those in their community who were as yet without Christ...and they were off!

Eric Barwick, one of the elders, tells of the growth of our bonding with the fellowship from its early seed-sowing in the 1950s:

Stanley Banks 'First My Friend'

My memories of Stanley go back to a day when he spoke at a rally in Chester to a group of lively young people, who nevertheless listened intently to a message clearly and simply presented. My next contact was when Stanley was the speaker at the Chester Convention. Again I was impressed by the clarity and directness of the ministry. My main memory remaining from that time is not so much his preaching as his praying. We met each night before the meeting for a short time of prayer, and Stanley was always there, sharing in that time, showing as he did so the great value he placed on prayer and revealing his own personal, intimate relationship with God by the way in which he prayed.

This was during the early days of the Waverton Fellowship, and it was not long after that it was suggested that Stanley be asked to preach for us. We thought it a great idea, but most of us were doubtful as to whether he would be able to fit us into his busy schedule. We were delighted when he did so and even more pleased when his visits took on a more regular pattern. His Bible teaching was a great blessing to us in those early days as the fellowship developed and we looked forward to his visits.

'We went on as a fellowship and were able to buy a disused Presbyterian Church in the village and, after a lot of work renovating and enlarging the premises, we were able to open the church for our regular services and general activities in October 1984.

When we were planning our opening services, the first choice of special preacher for that weekend was the Rev. Stanley Banks, and we were so glad that he was able to come to us for what was a very important day. He spoke so memorably, bringing us encouraging and challenging messages from God's Word which strengthened us and stirred us as we moved forward into a new place.

Perhaps the Waverton friends failed to realise that Stanley felt it an honour beyond anything he could

have wished for that they asked him to speak at the opening of a work which had become unspeakably dear to us both; and for him, it was a humbling experience to take a part in it.

Eric goes on: 'The fact that we were a small fellowship did not seem to make any difference to Stanley; he was used to the big occasion, the large crowd, the great auditorium, but was just as much at home with the small congregation, the handful of believers who were keen to learn from God's Word and be instructed in spiritual matters. For them there was just the same diligence and zeal as for the big convention.'

At this time the fellowship was changing from a system of leadership through a church council to that of elders and deacons, and during that transition period Eric remembers that Stanley 'was able to give counsel resulting from his wide experience and knowledge. It was a source of great strength and support to those taking on the responsibilities of leadership.'

How God touched the heart of one of the church elders to make available to us a beautiful cottage in the village of Great Barrow, not far from Waverton, is another story of God's provision for us both till Stanley went to his permanent home. Living in a village with its surrounding meadows, streams and cornfields was balm to his spirit as he returned to his roots—village life. He quickly acquainted himself with many of the footpaths surrounding Barrow, with the bowling green and its players, with the 'characters' who had lived for many years in the village, with Barrow's young rector who pastored the village church and whom Stanley discovered to be a true man of God. Many cups of coffee, prayer times and burdens were shared with John Hayes and his wife, Marion, during the two or three years we were part of the village life, and the friendship between the older man and his young brother in Christ became a firm and rewarding relationship.

Although Stanley's ministry continued to take him to many parts of the country, it was always with great joy that he returned to Waverton Evangelical Fellowship.

The commitment to the church was a 'real, practical expression of the teaching he had often given from the pulpit', Eric continues. 'It must have seemed strange at times for him to be sitting in the congregation when he was so used to being on the platform.' But, again, Eric didn't hear him say to me how much blessing he always received as he listened to one or other of our elders or deacons as they opened up the word.

> Whether on the platform or in the pew he was taking his part effectively in the body of Christ and functioning there in a way which brought encouragement to all in the fellowship. So it was not only on Sunday, but through the week at prayer meetings, or Bible study groups, he was always available to give advice and counsel, ready to spend time with individuals or groups, preparing material for Bible studies, contributing to the building up of the church.
>
> His own personal experience of the completeness of God's salvation brought such an assured and confident ring to his witness. The thrill of recounting the last words of Jesus on the cross, indicating as they did the fact that all the work he had come to do had been accomplished, shone through as Stanley shouted the Greek word, *Tetelastai*: It is finished!'

Stanley's appreciation of good physical health throughout his life was something he very often expressed to the Lord. Hardly ever did he need to cancel an appointment because of illness. There were times when he went in trepidation and weakness, due to minor ailments or migraine (from which he suffered for many years), but he was always delighted to tell me afterwards that during the giving of the word he was quite oblivious of any physical inhibition and knew only the sense of God's presence and unction.

In February 1962, however, following his first visit to South Africa, which had been extremely hectic in every way, Stanley suffered a minor heart strain and was prescribed a month's bed rest, followed by two months 'going slow'. He was a wonderfully patient patient, if a reluctant one! And during those (to him) rather long weeks of being 'out of the running' he had many precious times with his Lord—and of course the children and I saw more of him than we'd ever believed possible. But a statement in Psalm 23 became specially poignant to him in those days, through the ministry of a fellow worker in Emmanuel, the Rev. Adam Ritchie, who came and said, *'He maketh me to lie down...'* It wasn't the strenuous time he'd been through; it wasn't an unfortunate hiccup in his work schedule...it was the Lord's ordering. So Stanley learned that with God there are no second causes.

He made a complete recovery and by the autumn of the same year he was back in full harness and God gave him for many more years the privilege and responsibility of a full-time ministry.

Just before Easter 1989, he was preparing for a convention in which he had participated many times in previous years and one which always gave him great joy: the Faith Mission Convention in Bangor, Northern Ireland. He had to make an early start from Speke

Airport in Liverpool on the Good Friday, and I was to drive him there. So his case was packed in its usual orderly, immaculate style (he never allowed me to pack either for himself or for me; he was an expert!). So it was early to bed that Thursday night.

In the early hours of the morning he suffered a severe heart attack and a few hours later was taken to hospital in Chester; the telephone wires were busy as all the necessary rearrangements were made. Outwardly, Stanley appeared calm and at peace. The pain ceased and never returned. As I sat beside him in the ambulance I could only guess at his inner feelings, facing, as he did, a situation he had always feared, but the dynamic power he had proved so often in other circumstances was enabling him just then, in a completely new one, to cope, and continued to do so in the weary days that lay ahead.

He could never speak highly enough of the care and attention he received during that week in hospital and to all his visitors and to me he was always cheerful and full of praise, not only to the Lord but to the nurses 'who are marvellous and work so hard'.

But he had sustained permanent heart damage. His breathing was severely affected, and during the five months of weakness that followed he had to return to hospital twice more.

Our little home became a very sacred and special place, as we were able to spend so much time in each other's company, more than ever before. After he gained a little strength, he loved to walk around the village, up to the shop for his daily newspaper, or across to the bowling green, where, on his reappearance, one of his bowling pals greeted him with 'Eh, lad, it's good t'see you agen.'

But there were many days when he felt tremendous weariness of body, although never of spirit; for Stanley began, during these months, to delve deeper and deeper into the Book which was growing daily more vital and necessary to him. He was quite sure that the Lord was planning to heal him so that once again he could minister to others. He must prepare for that day. So he spent several hours every day studying the word and revelling in it, often tiring his mind and his hand as he wrote down his findings. And then he would find relaxation in the evening in games of Scrabble, or listening to his favourite records and tapes.

As the day drew near when he would again be able to preach, he said to me, 'God has given me so very much during these months that I have enough to give to last through the millenium!' And he became more and more impatient to begin again.

In October of the same year he preached again for the first time. It was in a small chapel in the lovely little town of Llangollen which nestles in a Welsh valley, a spot which had become very dear to him, a place where he had preached the word many times in recent years. And so once again he took off—longing for opportunities to share with others what had been given to him!

But he felt he was not doing enough; he had so much to give and, by his reckoning, not nearly enough opportunities to give it. One day early in 1990 he asked me to pray that the Lord would send him more invitations. 'I just long to tell out more of what the Lord has revealed to me.'

'Don't you think you're doing enough?' I asked, knowing pretty well what his answer would be—an unequivocal 'no.'

'OK,' I conceded. 'We'll pray that the Lord will send you just as many openings as he sees you can cope with.' And we did! And they came! And he didn't say 'no'.

How excited he was to be at it again! For the next four months practically every weekend was busy, and sometimes the week, too. One of his great joys was to be ministering again in his beloved Waverton and to share in the times of Bible study and prayer. St Bartholomew's Church in our own village of Great Barrow saw him in its pulpit early in January, at the request of his young friend, the rector, John Hayes. What a thrill this was to him!

Easter Sunday was spent in the church he pastored from 1942 to 1952, in the early days of service for the Lord: Emmanuel Church, Birkenhead. He enjoyed every moment of the time there, renewing fellowship with many friends of long-standing. It was hard to tear ourselves away after the evening service, for reminiscing is a deep joy when it is with those who have shared your life from its early days. In his message he joyfully proclaimed the Conquering Christ, the Companion Christ and the Commissioning Christ.

As the spring and early summer drew on he eagerly anticipated serving his Master in many different places, as his diary filled up. He was particularly looking forward to a May weekend in Kidderminster where he had shared often in recent years. Our younger daughter, Meryl, lived with her husband and family in nearby Worcester, so it was to be an exciting few days for more than one reason. The Sunday services were happy, fruitful times, and the Tuesday following included a picnic in Nunnery Wood with the family plus dog. What fun we had! Stanley had never seemed so well since his illness and was in great form, and how the little grand-daughters enjoyed the hilarity of games with Grandad!

Returning to our home in Great Barrow on the Wednesday, he took time to prepare for something he had looked forward to for weeks: the staff day of prayer at our OMS headquarters in Manchester. Early Thursday morning, the 17th of May, we drove over. What a wonderful day we all had! All of the British home staff gathered, and it was a blissfully happy time of renewed fellowship and friendship. Stanley spoke on 'Occupational Diseases', reminding us that salvation is a life that permeates, that the Holy Spirit uses a knife to prune, that he may bring about in our lives an overflow which produces fruit. He warned us to beware, in our personal lives, of professionalism, of staleness, of discouragement, of repenting our sacrifices, of overwork and of a lack of private devotional times; in our church to beware of a loss of distinctiveness, of inverted priorities, of a lack of commitment and of a lack of discipline. His final word to us at OMS staff day of prayer (and indeed to all of us who have sat under his ministry throughout his lifetime) was threefold: 'Listen to God. Look to God. Launch out for God.'

In less than twenty-four hours Stanley had reached heaven. How wonderful that God had granted him his request:

> Happy, if with my latest breath
> I might but grasp his name;
> Preach him to all and cry in death,
> 'Behold, behold the Lamb!'

It was just as he would have wished: no more invalidism; strength returned enough to preach to all—and then he was *home*.

His elder son, Ian, returning again to the family home on the day of the funeral, visited the chapel of rest to see his Dad for the last time. On coming back to the house, with awed voice he said, 'We didn't find him, Mum.'

No, the spirit had flown, and new feet were treading the halls of gold. Stuart, his younger son, brought us these words which he had found, author unknown:

This day in Paradise
new feet are treading through
high halls of gold.

This day in Paradise
new legs are striding over jewelled fields in which
the diamond
is considered ordinary.

This day in Paradise
new eyes have glimpsed the deep fire ready
to flame the stale earth pure.

This day in Paradise
new blood, the rose-red juice that gushed at Golgotha,
now ripples and races down the pure veins
of a recently arrived beloved.

This day in Paradise
a new heart pounds in praise,
a new body, shaped by sacrifice.

This day in Paradise
the daunting dart of death

has no point,
no place
and no meaning.

And while we mourn and weep
through these human hours,
This day in Paradise
the blazing embrace
between Saviour and son, goes on, and on, and on...

We found his instructions laid down for his funeral, meticulously as for everything else he did. He specified the hymns we were to sing, those who were to take part in the service at Waverton and (most revealing of all) that he should be buried in the small village churchyard at Great Barrow, showing what a special place it held in his heart. It was much more a time of thanksgiving and rejoicing for a life lived and coped with 'by his dynamic power' and for a pilgrim safely arrived on the further side: much more this, indeed, than a time of mourning and regret.

Gordon Taylor, Stanley's friend and colleague for many years, took us to the gates of heaven with John Bunyan; and I'd like to quote his words at length:

It was noised abroad that Mr Valiant for Truth was sent for by summons. When he understood it he called for his friends and told them of it. And then, said he, I am going to my fathers, and though with great difficulty I have got hither yet now do I not repent me of all the trouble I have been to arrive where I am. My sword I give to him that shall succeed me in my pilgrimage and my courage and skill to him than can get it; my marks and scars I carry with me to be a witness for me that I have fought his battles who now will be my Rewarder. When the day that he must go hence was come, many accompanied him to the riverside into the which as he went, he said, Death, where is thy sting? and as he went down deeper he said, Grave, where is thy victory? And so he passed over, and all the trumpets sounded for him on the other side....

Stanley Banks is not lost to us. Jesus said, 'Because I live, ye shall live also.' The believer lives! Well, of course there's natural sadness. And there are tears (and some of us are not very far from them now), and that's right! But I recall a favourite illustration of Stanley's (it must have been favourite because he told it on more than one occasion) [subdued chuckles at this point rippled through the congregation] how well he was known for his love of repeating his own favourite illustrations! (It's a good preacher when he knows it can stand repeating.) He told of a Salvation Army officer who was known for his faith and his love for Christ, and who suddenly hit tragedy when his son was taken dramatically and unexpectedly. A sceptic said to the officer, 'And what does your religion do for you now?' You remember the reply? He said, 'I'll tell you what my religion does for me: it enables me to shout Hallelujah! through my tears!' Now that, dear friends, is exactly what this service is all about. There are tears—there would be something wrong if there weren't! But through it all is a sense of triumph of the glory and the victory of the Lamb of God.

I was quite taken aback when Stanley spoke to me some time ago and invited me to take this position today. I count it a very great honour.

Stanley Banks was the last of six men who so much fashioned my own pilgrimage, and so in a sense it's the passing of an era for me personally, and I half suspect for some of you, and as someone commented recently, since his going, 'Yes, and the likes of him are not being easily replaced, in this generation.'

I have selected for my text today a rather neglected little phrase which Paul used of one of his colleagues. It is in Romans 16:10. He says, 'Salute Apelles, approved in

Christ!' That's all! What a wealth there is in that! We salute Stanley Banks today—approved in Christ! The word means tried and tested and found absolutely genuine. I don't think it's saying too much, is it, to say that as we survey this life of a man of God, it was approved in every kind of way.

I think that only as we ponder Stanley's life in retrospect shall we realise the enormous legacy he has left for us. Such a wide range of activity and experience: a principal and teacher, primarily of the word of God and the gospel of his Saviour; a minister and pastor to people, a counsellor to other leaders, a man to whom other ministers would go; an author, a broadcaster, an administrator, and, not least, a friend to all—and don't forget, what a friend said to me recently, 'and a thoroughly nice man, with it all'.

Will you allow me to say two things above all, for Christ, through the witness of this man? He was, primarily, a family man. You might be surprised at that, but listen! I'm thinking, of course, of his natural family. I don't think those of us who are not members of that family realise how much he could 'let his hair down' from time to time, and how much he endeared himself to every member of that family. And then the family of Emmanuel—a large family—and there are many of you here today, and your memories must go back over many years.

We can't over-emphasise the influence of Mr Banks, the strong natural leader, distinguishing himself so well as the leader of that large family, and the family of the OMS—his love for the worldwide missions. And then the family of a much wider church. For there are many across the world who have been touched by his ministry. And then the family of this local church. I know you speak of how much he meant to you, but you don't know how much you meant to him, and to the family to know that in their advancing years there was the lovely provision of accommodation, fellowship and ministry in this church here.

God gave Stanley Banks a graciousness to be able to straddle the divide which all too easily keeps even some of us evangelicals apart, and yet without compromising the great saving truths of the gospel of Christ.

Secondly, not only was he a family man, a teacher and preacher of the gospel, but he was also a gift of the Spirit to the church, to student and member of the fellowship of Christ alike, being able to explain so effectively and with such attractiveness the truths of God's word. I have often sat and coveted the way he could make profound things seemingly simple and eternal things so real and appealing. When a man makes it easy for many to love and serve Christ like that, then that's the mark of a true saint.

Dear friends, I don't know whether you realise what a specially significant day this is. It's Ascension Day! Could it be more appropriate? The Lord Jesus stands in the midst and says, 'I go to prepare a place for you.' Stanley is fortunate to have heard that and experienced it before any of us here. It's also another very special day that won't have escaped the memory of some. It's the very day of the anniversary of the Wesleys' conversion, the 24th May. And we realise, don't we, that it was this tradition from his earliest days, perhaps fashioned in Emmanuel, which he has followed in all his own pilgrimage and that moulded his own thinking and set his steps. And so it's very appropriate that we meet as we do today, to salute this veritable Apelles—approved unto God, in Christ, and in the holiness that he stood for, the holiness that he loved to preach, a central and dominant theme—he who lived holiness. But it wasn't the holiness of the halo on a man in a stained glass window, but the holiness of a man who made it attractive and happy, and who brought with him a sense of God, whether it was in a pulpit or in a home or in a classroom or on a convention platform, which he graced more times than we can count.

'Christ-centred, Bible-based, Spirit-filled—that summed up his life. There has passed from this earthly scene someone very special, and to us all who naturally feel sad at the earthly loss of a very great and unforgettable servant of God, I would say, let us remember the reason we rejoice today more than we mourn. The certainty of the gospel is the Resurrection; otherwise we would be of all men more miserable, but now is Christ risen from the dead and become the first to rise amongst those who sleep the sleep of death. Because Christ lives, Stanley lives, and the glory and the victory over the tomb belong to Stanley's Saviour and to ours. And all the praise and all the glory shall be to him in whom Stanley centred his life and to whom his faithful and able teaching always pointed.

The immeasurable loss to the church of Jesus on earth can only be matched by the immeasurable gain to the church of Jesus in heaven. And, dear friends, I can assure you that Stanley will be very much at home in heaven. To God be the glory!

So in the beautiful May sunshine we made our way to the churchyard on the hill at Great Barrow, surrounded by blossom and lush meadows. And we left just his shell there, while around the open grave we sang triumphantly, 'Thine be the glory, risen, conquering Son; endless is the victory Thou o'er death hast won.' For his spirit has indeed soared in triumph over the grave, and his life's influence will continue, because of that dynamic power, the power of the Resurrection, through which he always won the victory.

An illustration Stanley often gave was of an abortive attempt on Everest by Irving and Mallory. Through all difficulties, hazards and setbacks, they still climbed on and up. After no trace of them could be found, the last message sent back to Britain and round the world by the other team members was ' "Last seen, heading for the summit!" Will that be said of you and of me when we finish our earthly journey?' Stanley would ask.

It can surely be said of him: 'Last seen, heading for the summit!'